Especially for:

....

From:

....

Date:

....

My Daily Prayer Plan

2027 Edition

An Interactive Prayer Tracker for Women

BARBOUR
PUBLISHING™

YOU are the reason we do what we do here at Barbour Publishing. We promise that we will always use our God-given talents to produce content with you in mind—and that we will remain biblically faithful, no matter what.

Thank you for being the heart of our business.

Print ISBN 979-8-89151-361-7

Written by Annie Barkley and JoAnne Simmons.

Published by Barbour Publishing, Inc., 1810 Barbour Drive, Uhrichsville, Ohio 44683, www.barbourbooks.com

Our mission is to inspire the world with the life-changing message of the Bible.

ecpa Member of the Evangelical Christian Publishers Association

Printed in China.

Welcome to
My Daily Prayer Plan: 2027 Edition

What better way to start the new year than with a tool that can help your prayer life flourish in 2027? That's just what the book you hold in your hands can do.

Part daily devotional, part prayer journal, and part prayer tracker, this fantastic guide gives you everything you need to spend a few minutes every day with God—both in His Word and in prayer. Each day includes a scripture, devotional thought, and prayer starter. Then you'll be able to write down what's on your own heart in a conversation with God. (Don't worry about making your prayer perfect or eloquent. The Bible tells us in Jeremiah 29:12 that when we talk to God, He is faithful to listen.) At the bottom of the page are dedicated spots for your prayer requests, praises, and answers to prayer.

Each day of the week invites you to focus your prayers on the fruit of the Spirit (Galatians 5:22–23):

- Sunday: Love
- Monday: Joy
- Tuesday: Peace
- Wednesday: Patience and Kindness
- Thursday: Goodness
- Friday: Faithfulness
- Saturday: Gentleness and Self-Control

At the end of 2027, you'll have a year's worth of reflections to look back on and see how God has worked in your life. May this year be the next step in your faith journey as you come to know your heavenly Father more fully through prayer!

"When you pray, I will listen. If you look for me wholeheartedly, you will find me."
JEREMIAH 29:12–13 NLT

JANUARY 2027

"Teacher, which is the great commandment in the Law?"
MATTHEW 22:36 ESV

SUNDAY	MONDAY	TUESDAY	WEDNESDAY	THURSDAY	FRIDAY	SATURDAY
					1 New Year's Day	2
3	4	5	6	7	8	9
10	11	12	13	14	15	16
17	18 Martin Luther King Jr. Day	19	20	21	22	23
24 / 31	25	26	27	28	29	30

Are you starting the year with fresh determination and specific goals? Or are you just taking one day at a time as best you can? Either way, may all you do be rooted first and foremost in this: Love God with all your heart, soul, and mind. Second: Love your neighbor as yourself. There is no greater plan or purpose than to obey Jesus in these two—His *greatest*—commandments (Matthew 22:37–39)!

Friday, January 1

NEW YEAR'S DAY

Fear the Lord *and serve him faithfully with all your heart.*
For consider what great things he has done for you.
1 Samuel 12:24 ESV

Faithfully, with all my heart, Lord—that's how I want to fear You, honor You, love You, and serve You in this new year and all my life. Help me never forget all the great things You've done for me in the past, as I trust You for the present and the future.

PRAYER REQUESTS

ANSWERS TO PRAYER

PRAISES

Saturday, January 2

Again I say, don't get involved in foolish, ignorant arguments that only start fights. A servant of the Lord must not quarrel but must be kind to everyone, be able to teach, and be patient with difficult people. Gently instruct those who oppose the truth. Perhaps God will change those people's hearts, and they will learn the truth. Then they will come to their senses and escape from the devil's trap.

2 TIMOTHY 2:23–26 NLT

Lord, please help me to gently and wisely share Your truth. I pray that more and more people will let their hearts be changed by You!

PRAYER REQUESTS

ANSWERS TO PRAYER

PRAISES

Sunday, January 3

"When you obey my commandments, you remain in my love, just as I obey my Father's commandments and remain in his love. I have told you these things so that you will be filled with my joy. Yes, your joy will overflow! This is my commandment: Love each other in the same way I have loved you. There is no greater love than to lay down one's life for one's friends."

JOHN 15:10–13 NLT

Dear Jesus, You gave the perfect example and instructions on what love is and how to love others. Thank You! Please lead me in Your love and let it affect those around me.

PRAYER REQUESTS

PRAISES

ANSWERS TO PRAYER

Monday, January 4

Rejoice in the Lord always. I will say it again: Rejoice!
Let your gentleness be evident to all. The Lord is near.
PHILIPPIANS 4:4–5 NIV

It's not like You don't know that this life is hard, Lord. Still, Your Word tells us to rejoice always. You show us how to do that: by remembering You are near and praying to You about everything, with thanksgiving. You then give Your amazing peace—to replace our anxiety—as you guard our hearts and minds. Thank You!

ANSWERS TO PRAYER

PRAYER REQUESTS

PRAISES

Tuesday, January 5

I urge, then, first of all, that petitions, prayers, intercession and thanksgiving be made for all people—for kings and all those in authority, that we may live peaceful and quiet lives in all godliness and holiness.

1 TIMOTHY 2:1–2 NIV

Lord, I pray for all our leaders. Let them realize their need for Your wisdom above any human wisdom so they can help keep people in peace.

PRAYER REQUESTS

PRAISES

ANSWERS TO PRAYER

Wednesday, January 6

So let's not get tired of doing what is good. At just the right time we will reap a harvest of blessing if we don't give up. Therefore, whenever we have the opportunity, we should do good to everyone—especially to those in the family of faith.

GALATIANS 6:9–10 NLT

God, it's hard to be patient while I'm trying to do the right thing, and it's hard to wait on Your good results. Help me hang in there, please! I want to trust You and remember Your promises.

ANSWERS TO PRAYER

PRAYER REQUESTS

PRAISES

Thursday, January 7

She is clothed with strength and dignity, and she laughs without fear of the future. When she speaks, her words are wise, and she gives instructions with kindness. She carefully watches everything in her household and suffers nothing from laziness. . . . Charm is deceptive, and beauty does not last; but a woman who fears the LORD *will be greatly praised.*

PROVERBS 31:25–30 NLT

Lord, I'm thankful for the Proverbs 31 woman's example. Help me imitate her wisdom, kindness, and goodness.

PRAYER REQUESTS

ANSWERS TO PRAYER

PRAISES

Friday, January 8

Those who live in the shelter of the Most High will find rest in the shadow of the Almighty. This I declare about the LORD: He alone is my refuge, my place of safety; he is my God, and I trust him. . . . He will cover you with his feathers. He will shelter you with his wings. His faithful promises are your armor and protection.

PSALM 91:1–2, 4 NLT

Almighty God, I'm so grateful for the steadfast shelter, protection, and rest You faithfully provide. I want to help more people find unfailing refuge in You.

ANSWERS TO PRAYER

PRAYER REQUESTS

PRAISES

Saturday, January 9

Remind the believers to submit to the government and its officers. They should be obedient, always ready to do what is good. They must not slander anyone and must avoid quarreling. Instead, they should be gentle and show true humility to everyone.

Titus 3:1–2 NLT

Your ways of living are always best, Lord. Help me and all believers to obey Your instructions and conduct ourselves with gentleness and humility.

PRAYER REQUESTS

PRAISES

ANSWERS TO PRAYER

Sunday, January 10

Therefore I, a prisoner for serving the Lord, beg you to lead a life worthy of your calling, for you have been called by God. Always be humble and gentle. Be patient with each other, making allowance for each other's faults because of your love.
Ephesians 4:1–2 NLT

It's a challenge, for sure, to always be humble, gentle, and patient. Help me remember Paul's plea in this passage, Lord. It's so important to give grace to others for their faults. I certainly have my own faults, and I'm grateful when grace is given to me—especially the perfect, endless grace You give!

ANSWERS TO PRAYER

PRAYER REQUESTS

PRAISES

Monday, January 11

I know the Lord *is always with me. I will not be shaken, for he is right beside me. No wonder my heart is glad, and I rejoice. My body rests in safety. . . . You will show me the way of life, granting me the joy of your presence and the pleasures of living with you forever.*

Psalm 16:8–9, 11 NLT

Real, enduring joy comes from knowing You are always with me, always protecting me, always showing me the way of life. Thank You, Lord!

PRAYER REQUESTS

ANSWERS TO PRAYER

PRAISES

Tuesday, January 12

"I have said these things to you, that in me you may have peace. In the world you will have tribulation. But take heart; I have overcome the world."
John 16:33 ESV

Jesus, You don't sugarcoat things. You are honest that life is hard. Thank You for Your reminder that even during trial and suffering, I can find peace in You. I trust that You have overcome the world, and one day You'll redeem everything and make it all right.

ANSWERS TO PRAYER

PRAYER REQUESTS

PRAISES

Wednesday, January 13

He has told you, O man, what is good; and what does the Lord *require of you but to do justice, and to love kindness, and to walk humbly with your God?*
Micah 6:8 ESV

Lord, keep my focus on these good things You require of me. Show me ways to promote Your true justice. Help me choose kindness in all situations. Let me walk in close step with You every day.

PRAYER REQUESTS

ANSWERS TO PRAYER

PRAISES

Thursday, January 14

Finally, brothers and sisters, whatever is true, whatever is noble, whatever is right, whatever is pure, whatever is lovely, whatever is admirable—if anything is excellent or praiseworthy—think about such things. Whatever you have learned or received or heard from me, or seen in me—put it into practice.

PHILIPPIANS 4:8–9 NIV

Lord, keep reminding me of this wonderful scripture. If my mind is focused on goodness like Your Word instructs, then my actions will be too.

PRAYER REQUESTS

ANSWERS TO PRAYER

PRAISES

Friday, January 15

Trust in the L*ORD* *with all your heart; do not depend on your own understanding. Seek his will in all you do, and he will show you which path to take.*
PROVERBS 3:5–6 NLT

I often don't understand what You're doing, Lord. Help me to be faithful to You anyway. I know my understanding is flawed, and nothing is better than following You. Please lead me along the paths You have planned for me, step-by-step, day by day.

PRAYER REQUESTS

ANSWERS TO PRAYER

PRAISES

Saturday, January 16

The tongue is a small part of the body, but it makes great boasts. Consider what a great forest is set on fire by a small spark. The tongue also is a fire, a world of evil among the parts of the body. It corrupts the whole body, sets the whole course of one's life on fire, and is itself set on fire by hell.

James 3:5–6 NIV

Lord, help me. Constantly remind me of how important it is to keep control over my tongue.

PRAYER REQUESTS

ANSWERS TO PRAYER

PRAISES

Sunday, January 17

But if anyone has the world's goods and sees his brother in need,
yet closes his heart against him, how does God's love abide in him?
Little children, let us not love in word or talk but in deed and in truth.
1 John 3:17–18 ESV

Father God, open my eyes to the needs around me and help me meet them. I want to prove my love for You and others by what I do, in tangible ways that help care for people.

PRAYER REQUESTS

ANSWERS TO PRAYER

PRAISES

Monday, January 18

MARTIN LUTHER KING JR. DAY

A joyful heart is good medicine, but a crushed spirit dries up the bones.
PROVERBS 17:22 ESV

Please keep my heart joyful, Lord, no matter my circumstances. Help me focus on You in good times and bad. Happiness depends on situations, but real joy depends on Your presence. I have salvation in you, and I have Your Holy Spirit within me. I know You'll never leave or forsake me. I have every reason to rejoice!

ANSWERS TO PRAYER

PRAYER REQUESTS

PRAISES

Tuesday, January 19

You will keep in perfect peace all who trust in you, all whose thoughts are fixed on you! Trust in the LORD always, for the LORD GOD is the eternal Rock.

ISAIAH 26:3–4 NLT

Lord, I desperately need Your perfect peace. Everything feels so shaky right now. Remind me that You are the eternal Rock—solid, steady, and sure. I can certainly trust in You!

PRAYER REQUESTS

PRAISES

ANSWERS TO PRAYER

Wednesday, January 20

Be patient, then, brothers and sisters, until the Lord's coming.
See how the farmer waits for the land to yield its valuable crop,
patiently waiting for the autumn and spring rains. You too,
be patient and stand firm, because the Lord's coming is near.
JAMES 5:7–8 NIV

I want to wait on You well, Lord. Help me not to grow discouraged or whine while I wait. You have perfect timing and plans, and I want to stand firm and confident in my faith in You.

ANSWERS TO PRAYER

PRAYER REQUESTS

PRAISES

Thursday, January 21

"For I will change their sorrow to joy, and will comfort them. I will give them joy for their sorrow. I will fill the soul of the religious leaders with more than they need. My people will be filled with My goodness," says the Lord.

JEREMIAH 31:13–14 NLV

Lord, I long for heaven where there will be nothing but Your goodness to enjoy. But here on earth, while there are still troubles and sorrow, help me see Your blessings during the trials and focus on Your promises for the future.

PRAYER REQUESTS

PRAISES

ANSWERS TO PRAYER

Friday, January 22

"If you are faithful in little things, you will be faithful in large ones. But if you are dishonest in little things, you won't be honest with greater responsibilities. And if you are untrustworthy about worldly wealth, who will trust you with the true riches of heaven?"

LUKE 16:10–11 NLT

With anything You entrust to me, Lord, I want to be faithful. I want to obey and honor You in in the big things, the small things, and everything in between.

PRAYER REQUESTS

ANSWERS TO PRAYER

PRAISES

Saturday, January 23

"Come to me, all you who are weary and burdened, and I will give you rest. Take my yoke upon you and learn from me, for I am gentle and humble in heart, and you will find rest for your souls. For my yoke is easy and my burden is light."

Matthew 11:28–30 NIV

Lord, You know I need a soft place to land right now amid everything going on. Thank You for inviting all who are weary and burdened to come to You. I need You so much, especially the rest and peace You've promised.

PRAYER REQUESTS

ANSWERS TO PRAYER

PRAISES

Sunday, January 24

[Jesus said:] "Love each other. Just as I have loved you, you should love each other. Your love for one another will prove to the world that you are my disciples."
JOHN 13:34–35 NLT

Dear Jesus, remind us every day that the best way for Christians to prove that we trust and follow You is in the way we show love to one another. Help us sincerely seek Your love; fill us up so it overflows and points more people to You.

ANSWERS TO PRAYER

PRAYER REQUESTS

PRAISES

Monday, January 25

For I am not ashamed of this Good News about Christ. It is the power of God at work, saving everyone who believes—the Jew first and also the Gentile. This Good News tells us how God makes us right in his sight. This is accomplished from start to finish by faith.

ROMANS 1:16–17 NLT

Jesus, I don't ever want to feel ashamed of the good news of the gospel. Fill me with joy and eagerness to share with others about salvation from sin and eternal life in You. That's the best news ever!

PRAYER REQUESTS

ANSWERS TO PRAYER

PRAISES

Tuesday, January 26

"These things I have spoken to you while I am still with you. But the Helper, the Holy Spirit, whom the Father will send in my name, he will teach you all things and bring to your remembrance all that I have said to you. Peace I leave with you; my peace I give to you. Not as the world gives do I give to you. Let not your hearts be troubled, neither let them be afraid."

John 14:25–27 ESV

Lord, I'm so grateful for Your Holy Spirit, my helper. I'd be lost without You. Thank You for Your presence, peace, and love.

ANSWERS TO PRAYER

PRAYER REQUESTS

PRAISES

Wednesday, January 27

Do not let any unwholesome talk come out of your mouths,
but only what is helpful for building others up according
to their needs, that it may benefit those who listen.
EPHESIANS 4:29 NIV

Lord, help me be kind—not careless—with my words. I want to encourage and lift people up, not tear anyone down or be full of negativity and complaints.

PRAYER REQUESTS

PRAISES

ANSWERS TO PRAYER

Thursday, January 28

And we know that in all things God works for the good of those who love him, who have been called according to his purpose.

Romans 8:28 NIV

Only You, Lord, can take everything and work it all out for good for those who love You and have been called by You. I sure don't know how that's possible, but I know You do! I trust and love You completely.

ANSWERS TO PRAYER

PRAYER REQUESTS

PRAISES

Friday, January 29

I focus on this one thing: Forgetting the past and looking forward to what lies ahead, I press on to reach the end of the race and receive the heavenly prize for which God, through Christ Jesus, is calling us.
PHILIPPIANS 3:13–14 NLT

Dear Jesus, I pray for myself and all my brothers and sisters, because they love You too. May we always faithfully press on toward You!

PRAYER REQUESTS

PRAISES

ANSWERS TO PRAYER

Saturday, January 30

Never pay back evil with more evil. Do things in such a way that everyone can see you are honorable. Do all that you can to live in peace with everyone.
Romans 12:17–18 NLT

I'm upset, Lord. You know why. It's easy to want to retaliate and get revenge, but help me not to act on those feelings. Take them from me, and replace them with peace that overflows to everyone around me.

ANSWERS TO PRAYER

PRAYER REQUESTS

PRAISES

Sunday, January 31

Know therefore that the LORD your God is God, the faithful God who keeps covenant and steadfast love with those who love him and keep his commandments, to a thousand generations.

DEUTERONOMY 7:9 ESV

Lord God, Your love is steadfast and faithful, and I'm so thankful for it. Help me point others to Your love. Keep me within Your good boundaries and Your blessings as I seek to obey Your perfect commandments.

PRAYER REQUESTS

PRAISES

ANSWERS TO PRAYER

FEBRUARY 2027

This is the day that the Lord has made; we will rejoice and be glad in it.
Psalm 118:24 SKJV

SUNDAY	MONDAY	TUESDAY	WEDNESDAY	THURSDAY	FRIDAY	SATURDAY
	1	2	3	4	5	6
7	8	9	10 Ash Wednesday	11	12	13
14 Valentine's Day	15 Presidents' Day	16	17	18	19	20
21	22	23	24	25	26	27
28						

If you live somewhere in the northern hemisphere that enjoys all four seasons, February—the shortest month—can *feel* like the longest month, with frigid temperatures, snow, and ice. Still, every day is created by God, and each dawn gives us the chance to praise Him for all He has done and is yet to do!

Monday, February 1

"Ask and you will receive. Then your joy will be full."
JOHN 16:24 NLV

Father, I know Your Word says it's possible to live joyfully, but most of the time I feel like I just experience fleeting moments—short snippets—of joy. Teach me the secret of joy—that it's not based on a feeling but rather a deep, abiding faith that is anchored to Your steadfast love, protection, and beauty.

PRAYER REQUESTS

ANSWERS TO PRAYER

PRAISES

Tuesday, February 2

"Blessed are the peacemakers, for they will be called children of God."
Matthew 5:9 NIV

When I experience Your true peace, Lord, I feel what a blessing it is. I want more of it, and I want others to know the wonder of Your peace too! Show me how to be a peacemaker. Where there is conflict, let me be a voice of calm. Where there is anxiety, give me the tools to soothe and offer real hope. You are the giver of everlasting peace!

ANSWERS TO PRAYER

PRAYER REQUESTS

PRAISES

Wednesday, February 3

Don't run from tests and hardships, brothers and sisters. As difficult as they are, you will ultimately find joy in them; if you embrace them, your faith will blossom under pressure and teach you true patience as you endure. And true patience brought on by endurance will equip you to complete the long journey and cross the finish line—mature, complete, and wanting nothing.

James 1:2–4 VOICE

Lord, I will not run from the hard things You send my way. Please help me through tough times!

PRAYER REQUESTS

PRAISES

ANSWERS TO PRAYER

Thursday, February 4

Give thanks to the Lord for His loving-kindness and His great works to the children of men! For He fills the thirsty soul. And He fills the hungry soul with good things.
PSALM 107:8–9 NLV

You are my good, good Father, and I praise You for—well, *everything*! Everything I am, every talent I possess, every good gift You send my way is from You, Lord. Thank You for the big and small ways You work in my life.

ANSWERS TO PRAYER

PRAYER REQUESTS

PRAISES

Friday, February 5

For no matter how many promises God has made, they are "Yes" in Christ. And so through him the "Amen" is spoken by us to the glory of God.

2 Corinthians 1:20 NIV

Jesus, You are the fulfillment of so many of God's ancient promises. The fact that You did exactly what God required of You by laying down Your life for Your friends means that I can rely on God to fulfill His promises that are yet to come. You are God's ultimate "Yes!" and to that I say, "Amen!"

PRAYER REQUESTS

ANSWERS TO PRAYER

PRAISES

Saturday, February 6

Let the message about Christ, in all its richness, fill your lives.
Teach and counsel each other with all the wisdom he gives. Sing psalms
and hymns and spiritual songs to God with thankful hearts.
Colossians 3:16 NLT

I cherish Your Word, Father. Guide me to live in community with other believers who love the Bible, give sound wisdom and teaching from it, and uphold Your holy scripture as the living, breathing Word of God!

ANSWERS TO PRAYER

PRAYER REQUESTS

PRAISES

Sunday, February 7

Live a life filled with love, following the example of Christ. He loved us and offered himself as a sacrifice for us, a pleasing aroma to God.
EPHESIANS 5:2 NLT

I want my life to please You, Lord. I know You are cheering me on when I work to become kinder, more loving, more selfless, and more understanding—more like Your Son. Please encourage me to keep going when I mess up and remind me that Your grace covers my imperfections!

PRAYER REQUESTS

ANSWERS TO PRAYER

PRAISES

Monday, February 8

I pray that God, the source of hope, will fill you completely with joy and peace because you trust in him. Then you will overflow with confident hope through the power of the Holy Spirit.

Romans 15:13 NLT

I proclaim my confident hope in You today, Lord. I'm learning to trust You more and trust my feelings less (because they aren't reliable!). I may not be overflowing with joy this moment, but I believe with the power of the Holy Spirit, I will be soon!

PRAYER REQUESTS

ANSWERS TO PRAYER

PRAISES

Tuesday, February 9

Pursue peace with everyone, and holiness,
since no one will see God without it.
Hebrews 12:14 voice

Help me remember that pursuing peace is always worth the effort, God. If I let unkindness creep into my relationships and resentment take root, wake me up to the fact that these things are peace thieves and they have no place in my life. I will work toward peace with others and holiness within myself, Lord, as I pursue a deeper relationship with You.

PRAYER REQUESTS

ANSWERS TO PRAYER

PRAISES

Wednesday, February 10

ASH WEDNESDAY

"I know all the things you do. I have seen your love,
your faith, your service, and your patient endurance.
And I can see your constant improvement in all these things."
REVELATION 2:19 NLT

In Revelation 2, You're speaking to the church in Thyatira, Father. I want You to see these same things in me. Today I pray that I am faithful in my love, service to others, and patience. I pray for constant growth in my faith and relationship with You!

ANSWERS TO PRAYER

PRAYER REQUESTS

PRAISES

Thursday, February 11

O Lord, you are so good, so ready to forgive,
so full of unfailing love for all who ask for your help.
Psalm 86:5 NLT

Good seems like such an insignificant word to describe You, God, yet scripture calls You *good* again and again. Your goodness flows through Your love and plan of salvation. You sacrificed Your Son for my good and Your glory. You are my good helper and healer. You are good forever and ever, Father!

PRAYER REQUESTS

ANSWERS TO PRAYER

PRAISES

Friday, February 12

"I am leaving you with a gift—peace of mind and heart. And the peace I give is a gift the world cannot give. So don't be troubled or afraid."
JOHN 14:27 NLT

Jesus, Your sacrifice on the cross for my salvation was more than enough—but You didn't stop there. You cared so much for Your followers that You left us the gift of Your Spirit—the Holy Spirit that offers us peace. Wrap me in this peace today, Lord.

PRAYER REQUESTS

ANSWERS TO PRAYER

PRAISES

Saturday, February 13

Three things will last forever—faith, hope, and love—and the greatest of these is love.
1 Corinthians 13:13 NLT

Love is a superpower, and You are the greatest example of this, Father! Your love for me and for all Your creation is what makes my life—my very existence—possible. You forgive me because You love me. You discipline me because You love me. You comfort me because You love me. And You're preparing a place for me in heaven because You love me.

PRAYER REQUESTS

ANSWERS TO PRAYER

PRAISES

Sunday, February 14

VALENTINE'S DAY

May you have the power to understand, as all God's people should, how wide, how long, how high, and how deep his love is.
EPHESIANS 3:18 NLT

Lord, thank You for the gift of the deeply loving relationships in my life. Please be the center of these relationships so we can experience the vastness of Your love for us. Hold us and protect us in Your love. You, my God, are the very definition of *true love.*

ANSWERS TO PRAYER

PRAYER REQUESTS

PRAISES

Monday, February 15

PRESIDENTS' DAY

Be full of joy always because you belong to the Lord. Again I say, be full of joy!
PHILIPPIANS 4:4 NLV

I belong to You, Father! I am Your beloved child—an heir to Your kingdom and an essential member of Your church. You've made a home for me where I am now, but You're also preparing a place for me in heaven for all eternity. The whole world needs to experience that acceptance and the home I've found in Your heart!

PRAYER REQUESTS

PRAISES

ANSWERS TO PRAYER

Tuesday, February 16

Don't worry about anything; instead, pray about everything. Tell God what you need, and thank him for all he has done. Then you will experience God's peace, which exceeds anything we can understand. His peace will guard your hearts and minds as you live in Christ Jesus.

PHILIPPIANS 4:6–7 NLT

Father, right now I give You my worries in exchange for Your promise of peace. When worries try to creep back in, let that powerful peace banish those anxious thoughts!

ANSWERS TO PRAYER

PRAYER REQUESTS

PRAISES

Wednesday, February 17

"Those who show loving-kindness are happy, because they will have loving-kindness shown to them."
Matthew 5:7 NLV

Sometimes it's easy for me to be kind to others, Lord, but other times—well, on days when I'm tired, when I don't feel well, when the burdens of life weigh heavily on my spirit. . .kindness feels like a chore. In those moments, I need the help of the Holy Spirit to show love—because You are always so kind to me.

PRAYER REQUESTS

ANSWERS TO PRAYER

PRAISES

Thursday, February 18

Let all those redeemed by the Eternal—those rescued from times of deep trouble—join in giving thanks.

Psalm 107:2 voice

You are my rescuer, Lord—the one who saved me from my own selfish sin that would've ultimately led to death! Even when I face difficult times, You are there with me, helping me survive *and* thrive through even the hardest, scariest situations. Father, I am overflowing with gratitude for all You've done and are yet to do.

ANSWERS TO PRAYER

PRAYER REQUESTS

PRAISES

Friday, February 19

By his wounds you are healed.
1 PETER 2:24 NLT

The Bible tells me, Jesus, that as You got closer to the time of Your death, You struggled and grieved with what was coming. You even asked Your Father if there was some other way His plan of salvation could happen. But, loving Savior, You were faithful to submit to His will and the ridicule, persecution, torture, humiliation, and death. Now You are alive, and I'm alive in You!

PRAYER REQUESTS

ANSWERS TO PRAYER

PRAISES

Saturday, February 20

Do not spend time with heavy wine drinkers or those who gorge themselves on meat. For both the drunk and the glutton will end up broke, sleeping life away, and clothed in rags.
PROVERBS 23:20–21 VOICE

Father, sometimes I'm enticed to overindulge, overspend, overdo it. These temptations aren't inherently sinful, but my selfishness leads me to use them in sinful ways. Give me Your perspective, Lord, and help me practice self-control. If You want me to abstain entirely from something, help me learn that too.

ANSWERS TO PRAYER

PRAYER REQUESTS

PRAISES

Sunday, February 21

You do well when you obey the Holy Writings which say, "You must love your neighbor as you love yourself."
James 2:8 NLV

Show me, Father, practical ways to love others today—show me the needs You want me to meet in Your name. I admit that I am often too busy, too distracted, too self-absorbed to see the people You've put in my path. Open my eyes to see and love others the way You do, Father.

PRAYER REQUESTS

ANSWERS TO PRAYER

PRAISES

Monday, February 22

Even though you do not see [Jesus] now, you believe in him and are filled with an inexpressible and glorious joy, for you are receiving the end result of your faith, the salvation of your souls.

1 Peter 1:8–9 NIV

I am saved by Your grace, Lord! When I think about who I was before I met You, I'm overwhelmed with gratitude for what You're doing in my mind and heart. Thank You for making me whole, complete, and filled with Your joy.

ANSWERS TO PRAYER

PRAYER REQUESTS

PRAISES

Tuesday, February 23

Great peace have those who love your law;
nothing can make them stumble.
Psalm 119:165 ESV

It feels odd to say that I love rules, Lord, but when the rules are Your commandments, I am truly thankful for Your laws. When I obey Your expectations for my life, I live within guardrails that keep me from careening off Your path and suffering truly difficult consequences of my sins. I have peace in knowing that I'm headed in the right direction—following after You!

PRAYER REQUESTS

ANSWERS TO PRAYER

PRAISES

Wednesday, February 24

She opens her mouth with wisdom. The teaching of kindness is on her tongue.
PROVERBS 31:26 NLV

I want my life to be a classroom of kindness, Lord. I know others are watching—especially little ones. May the children in my life see me treat others the way I want to be treated. May words of encouragement, care, and Your wisdom roll off my tongue. Let my life be a reflection of Jesus.

ANSWERS TO PRAYER

PRAYER REQUESTS

PRAISES

Thursday, February 25

Let no corrupting talk come out of your mouths,
but only such as is good for building up, as fits the
occasion, that it may give grace to those who hear.
Ephesians 4:29 ESV

Remind me, God, that I can choose the trajectory of my words. Will my conversations add more hardness, more darkness to the world around me, or will my lips speak encouragement and grace? Help me choose good, fitting words that demonstrate Your love!

PRAYER REQUESTS

ANSWERS TO PRAYER

PRAISES

Friday, February 26

If you do not have wisdom, ask God for it. He is always ready to give it to you and will never say you are wrong for asking.
JAMES 1:5 NLV

God, my prayer list is often long with requests—big and small asks, trivial requests and weighty needs. I know You hear me and are faithful to answer, but I also know that sometimes what I *really* need is Your wisdom. So today, that's my first request: Please grant me wisdom, discernment, and understanding.

ANSWERS TO PRAYER

PRAYER REQUESTS

PRAISES

Saturday, February 27

He was oppressed, and he was afflicted, yet he opened not his mouth; like a lamb that is led to the slaughter, and like a sheep that before its shearers is silent, so he opened not his mouth.

Isaiah 53:7 ESV

When life's inevitable frustrations mount, Lord—when I want to snap back—help me remember that even as You endured the abuse and ridicule of the crucifixion, You did not retaliate. You remained silent. Give me the strength to do the same, patiently trusting in Your plan.

PRAYER REQUESTS

PRAISES

ANSWERS TO PRAYER

Sunday, February 28

Don't just pretend to love others. Really love them. Hate what is wrong. Hold tightly to what is good. Love each other with genuine affection, and take delight in honoring each other.
Romans 12:9–10 NLT

I want to have a pure heart toward others, Lord. Even when they have ulterior motives, I want only good for them. Make my love heartfelt and genuine. Take away my skepticism. Keep me from becoming jaded by darkness and instead be a light of Your love that shines for all to see.

PRAYER REQUESTS

ANSWERS TO PRAYER

PRAISES

MARCH 2027

"May the Lord *bless you and protect you. May the* Lord *smile on you and be gracious to you. May the* Lord *show you his favor and give you his peace."*
Numbers 6:24–26 NLT

SUNDAY	MONDAY	TUESDAY	WEDNESDAY	THURSDAY	FRIDAY	SATURDAY
	1	2	3	4	5	6
7	8	9	10	11	12	13
14 Daylight Saving Time Begins	15	16	17 St. Patrick's Day	18	19	20 First Day of Spring
21 Palm Sunday	22	23	24	25	26 Good Friday	27
28 Easter	29	30	31			

New weather, new life, new blooms, new blessings—there is so much to look forward to with springtime! Above all, let's honor the Lord, the Creator and giver of them all, as we ask for His blessing, protection, favor, and peace. May we feel the warmth of His smile upon us, His gracious goodness to us, every single day of our lives.

Monday, March 1

This is the day the Lord *has made. We will rejoice and be glad in it. . . .*
Give thanks to the Lord *for he is good! His faithful love endures forever.*
Psalm 118:24, 29 NLT

Your goodness is evident in every new day, Lord! Even if my circumstances aren't ideal, there is always a reason to praise and thank You, always a reason for joy because of Your presence. You are so good, so faithful, so loving—and I am in awe that I'm Yours!

ANSWERS TO PRAYER

PRAYER REQUESTS

PRAISES

Tuesday, March 2

Yet I still belong to you; you hold my right hand. You guide
me with your counsel, leading me to a glorious destiny.
Whom have I in heaven but you? I desire you more than anything
on earth. My health may fail, and my spirit may grow weak,
but God remains the strength of my heart; he is mine forever.
PSALM 73:23–26 NLT

Because You are the strength of my heart and You guide me, I have true peace. Thank You, Lord!

PRAYER REQUESTS

ANSWERS TO PRAYER

PRAISES

Wednesday, March 3

We long for our bodies to be released from sin and suffering. We, too, wait with eager hope for the day when God will give us our full rights as his adopted children, including the new bodies he has promised us. We were given this hope when we were saved. (If we already have something, we don't need to hope for it. But if we look forward to something we don't yet have, we must wait patiently and confidently.)

ROMANS 8:23–25 NLT

I look forward to all You have promised, Lord. Help me be patient and confident and bring honor to You while I wait.

ANSWERS TO PRAYER

PRAYER REQUESTS

PRAISES

Thursday, March 4

At the moment I have all I need—and more! I am generously supplied with the gifts you sent me with Epaphroditus. They are a sweet-smelling sacrifice that is acceptable and pleasing to God. And this same God who takes care of me will supply all your needs from his glorious riches, which have been given to us in Christ Jesus.

PHILIPPIANS 4:18–19 NLT

I ask that You provide this kind of goodness and blessing for the loved one who's on my mind right now, Lord. Please give them all they need plus more!

PRAYER REQUESTS

PRAISES

ANSWERS TO PRAYER

Friday, March 5

If we claim to be without sin, we deceive ourselves and the truth is not in us. If we confess our sins, he is faithful and just and will forgive us our sins and purify us from all unrighteousness.

1 John 1:8–9 NIV

Lord, thank You for letting me come to You again and again to confess my sin and receive grace, mercy, and peace. Thank You for being so faithfully forgiving. Help me be a faithful forgiver just like You when others sin against me.

ANSWERS TO PRAYER

PRAYER REQUESTS

PRAISES

Saturday, March 6

Dear brothers and sisters, if another believer is overcome by some sin, you who are godly should gently and humbly help that person back onto the right path. And be careful not to fall into the same temptation yourself. Share each other's burdens, and in this way obey the law of Christ.

GALATIANS 6:1–2 NLT

Lord, help me give mercy generously. I want to be someone who gently and humbly leads people back toward You when they've gone astray.

PRAYER REQUESTS

PRAISES

ANSWERS TO PRAYER

Sunday, March 7

Don't just pretend to love others. Really love them. Hate what is wrong. Hold tightly to what is good. Love each other with genuine affection, and take delight in honoring each other.

Romans 12:9–10 NLT

Lord, the word *love* gets thrown around so easily—and often counterfeitly. Help me to be genuine with love, in ways that match Your true love. Keep teaching me and growing me in Your perfect truth and ways.

ANSWERS TO PRAYER

PRAYER REQUESTS

PRAISES

Monday, March 8

Dear brothers and sisters, when troubles of any kind come your way, consider it an opportunity for great joy. For you know that when your faith is tested, your endurance has a chance to grow. So let it grow, for when your endurance is fully developed, you will be perfect and complete, needing nothing.

James 1:2–4 NLT

Remind me that troubles mean a chance to grow in greater faith and dependence on You, Lord. And that's where I find greater joy too. The greater my faith and reliance on You, the better off I truly am.

PRAYER REQUESTS

ANSWERS TO PRAYER

PRAISES

Tuesday, March 9

Work at living in peace with everyone, and work at living a holy life, for those who are not holy will not see the Lord.
HEBREWS 12:14 NLT

Lord, remind me that real peace doesn't happen from doing nothing. It can take some serious work to resolve conflict, develop understanding, and extend forgiveness and grace to others. Please give me wisdom as I seek to live in peace with everyone.

PRAYER REQUESTS

ANSWERS TO PRAYER

PRAISES

Wednesday, March 10

Once safely on shore, we found out that the island was called Malta. The islanders showed us unusual kindness. They built a fire and welcomed us all because it was raining and cold.

Acts 28:1–2 NIV

Lord, I want to be known for unusual kindness. I want Your love to flow through me and pour out of me. Show me practical things I can do for those around me to help meet needs and offer encouragement and compassion.

PRAYER REQUESTS

ANSWERS TO PRAYER

PRAISES

Thursday, March 11

Every good and perfect gift is from above, coming down from the Father of the heavenly lights, who does not change like shifting shadows.
James 1:17 NIV

I praise You for every good thing, Lord! Every blessing comes ultimately from You. I'm so grateful for Your unchanging presence in my life. I want to share all the goodness You've given me with others so they'll love and follow You too.

PRAYER REQUESTS

ANSWERS TO PRAYER

PRAISES

Friday, March 12

Dear friend, I pray that you may enjoy good health and that all may go well with you, even as your soul is getting along well. It gave me great joy when some believers came and testified about your faithfulness to the truth, telling how you continue to walk in it. I have no greater joy than to hear that my children are walking in the truth.

3 John 1:2–4 NIV

Lord, I hope it's said of me that I am always faithful to Your truth. Please keep me in close step with You all my life.

PRAYER REQUESTS

PRAISES

ANSWERS TO PRAYER

Saturday, March 13

Understand this, my dear brothers and sisters: You must all be quick to listen, slow to speak, and slow to get angry. Human anger does not produce the righteousness God desires.

James 1:19–20 NLT

Lord, You know how much I need self-control with anger sometimes. Forgive me when I let it get the best of me. Help me remember the wisdom of Your Word and that I always need to be quick to listen, slow to speak, and slow to get angry.

ANSWERS TO PRAYER

PRAYER REQUESTS

PRAISES

Sunday, March 14

DAYLIGHT SAVING TIME BEGINS

"If you love those who love you, what credit is that to you? . . . But love your enemies, do good to them, and lend to them without expecting to get anything back. Then your reward will be great, and you will be children of the Most High, because he is kind to the ungrateful and wicked. Be merciful, just as your Father is merciful."

Luke 6:32–36 NIV

Dear Jesus, the challenge of Your command in this passage often feels impossible, but I trust You to teach me and to help me obey it.

PRAYER REQUESTS

ANSWERS TO PRAYER

PRAISES

Monday, March 15

I have spoken to you with great frankness; I take great pride in you.
I am greatly encouraged; in all our troubles my joy knows no bounds.
2 Corinthians 7:4 niv

Lord, surround me with fellow believers who encourage me despite all my troubles. Let us motivate one another to fix our eyes on You through the trials. Remind us of the real joy You provide. Let us delight in it, even during struggle, sorrow, and pain.

ANSWERS TO PRAYER

PRAYER REQUESTS

PRAISES

Tuesday, March 16

In peace I will lie down and sleep,
for you alone, O Lord, will keep me safe.
Psalm 4:8 NLT

You know how much I need rest right now, Lord. I ask You to bless me with supernaturally good sleep, full of the peace that comes from You alone. I trust in Your care, Your protection, and the good plans You have for my life.

PRAYER REQUESTS

ANSWERS TO PRAYER

PRAISES

Wednesday, March 17

ST. PATRICK'S DAY

Keep on loving one another as brothers and sisters. Do not forget to show hospitality to strangers, for by so doing some people have shown hospitality to angels without knowing it. Continue to remember those in prison as if you were together with them in prison, and those who are mistreated as if you yourselves were suffering.

HEBREWS 13:1–3 NIV

Lord, let me bless and help provide for someone in need today. Show me exactly who, where, and when.

ANSWERS TO PRAYER

PRAYER REQUESTS

PRAISES

Thursday, March 18

Do good to your servant according to your word, Lord.
Teach me knowledge and good judgment, for I trust your commands.
Before I was afflicted I went astray, but now I obey your word.
You are good, and what you do is good; teach me your decrees.
Psalm 119:65–68 NIV

I love that straightforward statement, Lord: You are good and You do what is good. There is nothing better I can do than love You, learn from You, and imitate You!

PRAYER REQUESTS

PRAISES

ANSWERS TO PRAYER

Friday, March 19

Sing joyfully to the LORD, you righteous; it is fitting for the upright to praise him. Praise the LORD with the harp; make music to him on the ten-stringed lyre. Sing to him a new song; play skillfully, and shout for joy. For the word of the LORD is right and true; he is faithful in all he does.

PSALM 33:1–4 NIV

You are faithful in all You do, Lord. I worship You. I want to keep growing to become more and more like You!

PRAYER REQUESTS

ANSWERS TO PRAYER

PRAISES

Saturday, March 20

FIRST DAY OF SPRING

Live wisely among those who are not believers, and make the most of every opportunity. Let your conversation be gracious and attractive so that you will have the right response for everyone.

Colossians 4:5–6 NLT

Lord, please give me wisdom when talking to unbelievers. Help me gently urge them to know and love You as Savior through gracious and attractive conversations.

PRAYER REQUESTS

ANSWERS TO PRAYER

PRAISES

Sunday, March 21

PALM SUNDAY

Imitate God, therefore, in everything you do, because you are his dear children. Live a life filled with love, following the example of Christ. He loved us and offered himself as a sacrifice for us, a pleasing aroma to God.

EPHESIANS 5:1–2 NLT

Dear God, it's easy to get caught up in the ways of the world, so please help me avoid that temptation. I want to imitate You, especially by loving others like Jesus did.

PRAYER REQUESTS

ANSWERS TO PRAYER

PRAISES

Monday, March 22

Weeping may last through the night, but joy comes with the morning.
PSALM 30:5 NLT

Sometimes I need reminders that sorrow and tears are not forever, Lord. Please fill me with the joy of Your presence. Comfort me and give me peace. Let those around me encourage me with Your love and truth. Thank You!

PRAYER REQUESTS

ANSWERS TO PRAYER

PRAISES

Tuesday, March 23

"Don't be afraid, for I am with you. Don't be discouraged, for I am your God. I will strengthen you and help you. I will hold you up with my victorious right hand."
Isaiah 41:10 NLT

Lord, You are the constant, steadying source of strength in my life—the reason I can have peace amid any storm. I am so grateful for You!

ANSWERS TO PRAYER

PRAYER REQUESTS

PRAISES

Wednesday, March 24

Then people brought little children to Jesus for him to place his hands on them and pray for them. But the disciples rebuked them. Jesus said, "Let the little children come to me, and do not hinder them, for the kingdom of heaven belongs to such as these."
MATTHEW 19:13–14 NIV

Lord, children hold a special place in Your heart. Help me always be extra patient and kind with the littles ones in my life.

PRAYER REQUESTS

PRAISES

ANSWERS TO PRAYER

Thursday, March 25

For God called you to do good, even if it means suffering, just as Christ suffered for you. He is your example, and you must follow in his steps. He never sinned, nor ever deceived anyone. He did not retaliate when he was insulted, nor threaten revenge when he suffered. He left his case in the hands of God, who always judges fairly.

1 PETER 2:21–23 NLT

Dear Jesus, help me be steadfast and strong in doing good, even if it means suffering here on earth. I believe that You will make all things just and right one day soon.

PRAYER REQUESTS

ANSWERS TO PRAYER

PRAISES

Friday, March 26

GOOD FRIDAY

He humbled himself in obedience to God and died a criminal's death on a cross. Therefore, God elevated him to the place of highest honor and gave him the name above all other names.
PHILIPPIANS 2:8–9 NLT

Dear Jesus, because of Your humble, faithful obedience to the Father, You died on the cross to provide a way for salvation from sin. I can't ever thank You enough for Your sacrifice. Now You are alive, and I lift Your great name high!

PRAYER REQUESTS

ANSWERS TO PRAYER

PRAISES

Saturday, March 27

In a wealthy home some utensils are made of gold and silver, and some are made of wood and clay. The expensive utensils are used for special occasions, and the cheap ones are for everyday use. If you keep yourself pure, you will be a special utensil for honorable use. Your life will be clean, and you will be ready for the Master to use you for every good work.

2 Timothy 2:20–21 NLT

Lord, I want to always practice good self-control and keep myself pure so I can be ready to accomplish the most honorable things for You!

ANSWERS TO PRAYER

PRAYER REQUESTS

PRAISES

Sunday, March 28

EASTER

God showed how much he loved us by sending his one and only Son into the world so that we might have eternal life through him. This is real love—not that we loved God, but that he loved us and sent his Son as a sacrifice to take away our sins. Dear friends, since God loved us that much, we surely ought to love each other.

1 John 4:9–11 NLT

Dear Jesus, thank You for suffering on the cross to take the punishment for my sin. I love You and am so grateful for You, my risen, living Savior!

PRAYER REQUESTS

ANSWERS TO PRAYER

PRAISES

Monday, March 29

Let your face smile on us, Lord. *You have given me greater joy than those who have abundant harvests of grain and new wine. In peace I will lie down and sleep, for you alone, O* Lord, *will keep me safe.*

Psalm 4:6–8 NLT

Lord, remind me that all the temporary delights of this world are nothing compared to the lasting joy, peace, and security that You alone can give. Please bless me and smile upon me every day of my life.

PRAYER REQUESTS

ANSWERS TO PRAYER

PRAISES

Tuesday, March 30

Now may the Lord of peace himself give you his peace at all times and in every situation. The Lord be with you all.
2 Thessalonians 3:16 NLT

Dear Jesus, You know the hard situation I'm thinking of right now. Help me and everyone involved to remember that You are the Lord of peace. Please give Your supernatural peace at all times, and let us feel Your presence. Thank You!

PRAYER REQUESTS

PRAISES

ANSWERS TO PRAYER

Wednesday, March 31

He gives power to the weak and strength to the powerless. Even youths will become weak and tired, and young men will fall in exhaustion. But those who trust in the LORD will find new strength. They will soar high on wings like eagles. They will run and not grow weary. They will walk and not faint.

ISAIAH 40:29–31 NLT

I feel so weary, Lord. Remind me of Your Word. and help me wait patiently for Your new strength to fill me at exactly the right time.

PRAYER REQUESTS

ANSWERS TO PRAYER

PRAISES

APRIL 2027

Do not forget to rejoice, for hope is always just around the corner. Hold up through the hard times that are coming, and devote yourselves to prayer.
ROMANS 12:12 VOICE

SUNDAY	MONDAY	TUESDAY	WEDNESDAY	THURSDAY	FRIDAY	SATURDAY
				1	2	3
4	5	6	7	8	9	10
11	12	13	14	15	16	17
18	19	20	21 Passover Begins at Sundown	22	23	24
25	26	27	28	29	30	

No matter what you're facing today, this week, this month, or this year, your Father is right there with you. When it's difficult to praise God because of your circumstances, double down, hold on to hope, and as Romans 12:12 says, continue to devote yourself to prayer!

Thursday, April 1

"No one lights a lamp and then puts it under a basket. Instead, a lamp is placed on a stand, where it gives light to everyone in the house. In the same way, let your good deeds shine out for all to see, so that everyone will praise your heavenly Father."

MATTHEW 5:15–16 NLT

I want to do good in Your name, Father. I will lay down my desire for praise and instead point to You as the source of all good things.

ANSWERS TO PRAYER

PRAYER REQUESTS

PRAISES

Friday, April 2

O Lord God of Heaven's Armies! Where is there anyone as mighty as you, O Lord? You are entirely faithful.
Psalm 89:8 NLT

I never have to worry and wonder about ulterior motives with You, Lord. You are faithful and true to who You are—always working to bring about Your kingdom. You long for every heart to be saved and sanctified. Your plan is to bring wholeness and healing to Your beloved creation.

PRAYER REQUESTS

ANSWERS TO PRAYER

PRAISES

Saturday, April 3

If you are angry, do not let it become sin. Get over your anger before the day is finished. Do not let the devil start working in your life.

EPHESIANS 4:26–27 NLV

Satan's tricks and schemes are so predictable, yet I often fall for them, straight into sin. Open my eyes, make me vigilant, and keep me safe from the devil's traps. I know You are faithful to provide an escape from temptation (1 Corinthians 10:13).

PRAYER REQUESTS

ANSWERS TO PRAYER

PRAISES

Sunday, April 4

The Lord Who made you, O Jacob, and He Who made you, O Israel, says, "Do not be afraid. For I have bought you and made you free. I have called you by name. You are Mine!"
ISAIAH 43:1 NLV

What a blessing it is to belong to You, Father! I am Your beloved child. You formed me and loved me into life, but you didn't stop there. You made a way for me to be with You forever through Jesus' sacrifice on the cross. Hallelujah!

PRAYER REQUESTS

ANSWERS TO PRAYER

PRAISES

Monday, April 5

Don't run from tests and hardships, brothers and sisters. As difficult as they are, you will ultimately find joy in them; if you embrace them, your faith will blossom under pressure and teach you true patience as you endure.

JAMES 1:2–3 VOICE

Lord, Your Word says that joy can be found in trials, and I believe what You say. But it's all but impossible for me to welcome difficult times. Show me how to grow during hardships into what You want me to be.

PRAYER REQUESTS

ANSWERS TO PRAYER

PRAISES

Tuesday, April 6

Those who plant seeds of peace will gather what is right and good.
JAMES 3:18 NLV

Living peacefully has its own reward, God, but Your Word promises that promoting peace around me will result in even more goodness! Peace leads to harmony, right living, deeper connection with others, and a sense of well-being. When others notice something different about my life, I will point them to You, the giver of lasting peace.

PRAYER REQUESTS

PRAISES

ANSWERS TO PRAYER

Wednesday, April 7

Since you are all set apart by God, made holy and dearly loved, clothe yourselves with a holy way of life: compassion, kindness, humility, gentleness, and patience.
Colossians 3:12 voice

Since You adopted me into Your family, Father, the dark world can no longer claim me as one of them. I want others to see me as different—in the best way possible—from the world. I will work to display more empathy, meekness, patience, and love. Let me be more like You every day!

ANSWERS TO PRAYER

PRAYER REQUESTS

PRAISES

Thursday, April 8

Then God looked over all he had made,
and he saw that it was very good!
Genesis 1:31 NLT

Thank You, Lord, for displaying Your goodness in creation. The seasonal cycles of trees and plants show me that You delight in rebirth and renewal. The horizon is the canvas for Your paintbrush to craft beautiful sunrises, assuring me that Your mercies are new every morning. The melody of a child's laughter assures me that You delight in a pure heart and simple faith.

PRAYER REQUESTS

ANSWERS TO PRAYER

PRAISES

Friday, April 9

"The master was full of praise. 'Well done, my good and faithful servant. You have been faithful in handling this small amount, so now I will give you many more responsibilities. Let's celebrate together!'"
MATTHEW 25:21 NLT

You have given me so much, Lord, and I want to use everything I have wisely and for Your glory. You have always been faithful to provide for me, and I will be faithful in taking care of all these good blessings by blessing others.

ANSWERS TO PRAYER

PRAYER REQUESTS

PRAISES

Saturday, April 10

Don't you realize that in a race everyone runs,
but only one person gets the prize? So run to win!
1 Corinthians 9:24 NLT

I'm saved by Your grace alone, Father, but I also want my journey of faith to be one of growth, of maturing, of learning to love You and trust You more. So I will run this race of faith to the best of my ability—knowing You are there, cheering me on, and will reward me with the prize of eternity with You!

PRAYER REQUESTS

ANSWERS TO PRAYER

PRAISES

Sunday, April 11

Brothers and sisters, God has called you to freedom! Hear the call, and do not spoil this gift by using your liberty to engage in what your flesh desires; instead, use it to serve each other as Jesus taught through love.

Galatians 5:13 voice

Because of Your grace, Lord, I am free from the burden of keeping every Old Testament law. Today, instead of serving myself, I choose to use that freedom to serve others. Help me become more like Jesus.

ANSWERS TO PRAYER

PRAYER REQUESTS

PRAISES

Monday, April 12

You have given me greater joy than those who have abundant harvests of grain and new wine. In peace I will lie down and sleep, for you alone, O Lord, will keep me safe.

Psalm 4:7–8 NLT

I see so much hopelessness around me, Lord, and it breaks my heart. Today I am thankful for the hope and joy I have because of You. I will shine Your light of hope into the world around me.

PRAYER REQUESTS

PRAISES

ANSWERS TO PRAYER

Tuesday, April 13

Deceit is in the hearts of those who plot evil,
but those who promote peace have joy.
PROVERBS 12:20 NIV

The world is full of people who wish harm and chaos on others, but with Your help, Father, I want to spread peace and wholeness to everyone around me. Your peace fills me with confidence in Your plans and hope for the future, because You are there—working all things together for my good and Your glory.

ANSWERS TO PRAYER

PRAYER REQUESTS

PRAISES

Wednesday, April 14

Your kindness will reward you, but your cruelty will destroy you.
PROVERBS 11:17 NLT

Lord, I want to be kind to others because You are so kind to me. In those moments when my own selfishness rears up and my knee-jerk reaction is to be mean, remind me that cruelty only leads to difficulties—now and in the future. I want to be a mender, not a destroyer. Thank You for giving me the very best example of this!

PRAYER REQUESTS

ANSWERS TO PRAYER

PRAISES

Thursday, April 15

Do not be overcome by evil, but overcome evil with good.
Romans 12:21 NIV

You give me the ability to *choose* to do good, no matter the circumstance, Father! Even when I am tempted to do wrong, give me the discipline to turn my back on evil's darkness so I am fully facing Your light and goodness. Then I'll be able to confidently walk ahead, and with Your help, we will overcome evil and the devil himself!

ANSWERS TO PRAYER

PRAYER REQUESTS

PRAISES

Friday, April 16

The Lord is faithful. He will give you strength and keep you safe from the devil.

2 Thessalonians 3:3 NLV

Today is a day when I need a little extra strength, Lord. Will You please hold me up in Your mighty arms? Challenges feel a little more difficult, and my soul is heavy. If this is Satan's work to frustrate me, I know You are faithful to defend me, keep me safe, and restore me to wholeness. We are in this together, Father!

PRAYER REQUESTS

ANSWERS TO PRAYER

PRAISES

Saturday, April 17

Better to be patient than powerful; better to have self-control than to conquer a city.
PROVERBS 16:32 NLT

God, it's difficult to pray for patience, because truthfully, I don't want to be put in a situation where I must put it into practice. But You rank patience as a key characteristic—an attribute that comes from the Holy Spirit. So Lord, if You say patience and self-control are the best things for me right now, then I am willing to learn.

ANSWERS TO PRAYER

PRAYER REQUESTS

PRAISES

Sunday, April 18

Let me hear of your unfailing love each morning, for I am trusting you. Show me where to walk, for I give myself to you.
PSALM 143:8 NLT

Some mornings I wake up singing Your praises, Lord, but others. . .well, not so much. On those days when I feel unsure, anxious, worried, unworthy, unwanted, or fearful, please let me hear You sing a love song over me. Guide me as my good shepherd, and I will follow where You lead.

PRAYER REQUESTS

ANSWERS TO PRAYER

PRAISES

Monday, April 19

If some have cause to celebrate, join in the celebration.
And if others are weeping, join in that as well.
ROMANS 12:15 VOICE

It's easy to fall into the habit of living a solitary life, Lord. I go through my days seeing the same people, having the same surface-level conversations. But You call me to deeper, more meaningful relationships. Help me to really know what's going on with others so I can rejoice with them when they rejoice and weep when they weep.

PRAYER REQUESTS

ANSWERS TO PRAYER

PRAISES

Tuesday, April 20

"For the mountains may depart and the hills be removed, but my steadfast love shall not depart from you, and my covenant of peace shall not be removed," says the L*ORD*, *who has compassion on you.*

ISAIAH 54:10 ESV

Father, I praise You for being the covenant-keeping God! I never have to wonder whether You love me or whether Your peace is available to me. Your love and Your peace are forever, and I will always seek them.

PRAYER REQUESTS

ANSWERS TO PRAYER

PRAISES

Wednesday, April 21

PASSOVER BEGINS AT SUNDOWN

Love is patient; love is kind. Love isn't envious, doesn't boast, brag, or strut about. There's no arrogance in love; it's never rude, crude, or indecent—it's not self-absorbed. Love isn't easily upset. Love doesn't tally wrongs.

1 Corinthians 13:4–5 voice

Your love for me is perfect, Father! You have no ulterior motives in showing me that You love me—total love is simply who You are. Help me love others with this same pure, authentic, humble love.

ANSWERS TO PRAYER

PRAYER REQUESTS

PRAISES

Thursday, April 22

Do not allow this world to mold you in its own image. Instead, be transformed from the inside out by renewing your mind. As a result, you will be able to discern what God wills and whatever God finds good, pleasing, and complete.
Romans 12:2 voice

I look to You, Jesus, as my role model in all ways. Please transform the way I think to be like You. I want to become like You more and more each day.

PRAYER REQUESTS

ANSWERS TO PRAYER

PRAISES

Friday, April 23

Jesus Christ is the same yesterday, today, and forever.
HEBREWS 13:8 NLT

People often tell me how much I look like my mom—how much they are reminded of her when they see me. Jesus, You are made from the same stuff as Your Father too! God is never ending and steadfast and faithful and unchanging—and so are You. I am thankful to have a Father *and* a Brother I can rely on no matter what.

ANSWERS TO PRAYER

PRAYER REQUESTS

PRAISES

Saturday, April 24

Guard your words, mind what you say,
and you will keep yourself out of trouble.
Proverbs 21:23 voice

Father, I need Your help putting my words through a filter before I say them. I will continue to pray and meditate on Your scripture regularly so my mind can act as that filter to help me choose helpful, uplifting, and encouraging words. It's *Your* wise words that I want to come out of my mouth, Lord!

PRAYER REQUESTS

ANSWERS TO PRAYER

PRAISES

Sunday, April 25

So who can separate us? What can come between us and the love of God's Anointed? Can troubles, hardships, persecution, hunger, poverty, danger, or even death? The answer is, absolutely nothing.

ROMANS 8:35 VOICE

Your love for me, Father, will go on forever. You have loved me from the time You first thought of me, from the moment You formed me in my mother's womb. No person, no spirit, no disaster will stand in the way of Your love for me!

ANSWERS TO PRAYER

PRAYER REQUESTS

PRAISES

Monday, April 26

Let all who take refuge in you be glad; let them ever sing for joy. Spread your protection over them, that those who love your name may rejoice in you.

Psalm 5:11 niv

Your Word tells me that You are my protector, God, and I trust You to keep me safe. When I feel weak or vulnerable, I will rely on You. And when the threat is over, I will sing Your praises, because You are my good, good Father!

PRAYER REQUESTS

PRAISES

ANSWERS TO PRAYER

Tuesday, April 27

Finally, brothers and sisters, rejoice! Strive for full restoration, encourage one another, be of one mind, live in peace. And the God of love and peace will be with you.

2 Corinthians 13:11 NIV

Thriving, life-giving, God-honoring relationships are what I want with the people around me, Father! If there is anyone I am at odds with, show me how to bring us to full restoration and at peace with each other. I will infuse Your encouragement into my conversations and interactions today, Lord.

ANSWERS TO PRAYER

PRAYER REQUESTS

PRAISES

Wednesday, April 28

When someone does something bad to you, do not do the same thing to him. When someone talks about you, do not talk about him. Instead, pray that good will come to him. You were called to do this so you might receive good things from God.

1 Peter 3:9 NLV

Lord, when someone has a problem with me, I will pray and ask You to help them and bless them. Because You know what they—and I—need.

PRAYER REQUESTS

PRAISES

ANSWERS TO PRAYER

Thursday, April 29

Everything God made is good. We should not put anything aside if we can take it and thank God for it.

1 Timothy 4:4 NLV

Your blessings surround me every day, Father—so many good things that I can't even see or acknowledge them all. Open my eyes to Your blessings and help me embrace them, both the big things and the small. Thank You for loving me so much that You delight in giving me good things, Father!

PRAYER REQUESTS

ANSWERS TO PRAYER

PRAISES

Friday, April 30

Count on this: God is faithful and in His faithfulness called you out into an intimate relationship with His Son, our Lord Jesus the Anointed.

1 Corinthians 1:9 voice

I am learning how to trust You more each day, Lord. I believe every scripture that proclaims Your faithfulness, and the longer I believe it, the more I experience it. It's such a blessed relief to know that You've never failed me yet and You won't start now.

PRAYER REQUESTS

PRAISES

ANSWERS TO PRAYER

MAY 2027

Devote yourselves to prayer with an alert mind and a thankful heart.
COLOSSIANS 4:2 NLT

SUNDAY	MONDAY	TUESDAY	WEDNESDAY	THURSDAY	FRIDAY	SATURDAY
						1
2	3	4	5	6 National Day of Prayer	7	8
9 Mother's Day	10	11	12	13	14	15
16	17	18	19	20	21	22
23 / 30	24 / Memorial Day 31	25	26	27	28	29

It's wonderful to have a National Day of Prayer on the calendar. May it urge more and more people to be humble before almighty God, remembering how great our need is for Him and how He is sovereign over everything. As more people draw closer to Him, may we all be devoted to prayer every day, every hour, every moment.

Saturday, May 1

A person's wisdom yields patience; it is to one's glory to overlook an offense.
Proverbs 19:11 NIV

Dear Lord, help me to use good self-control and choose battles wisely. I don't want to have conflict over small things. Teach me to let go of offenses and forgive quickly and easily. You will bring people to justice; that's not my job. I trust You!

PRAYER REQUESTS

ANSWERS TO PRAYER

PRAISES

Sunday, May 2

Nothing can ever separate us from God's love. Neither death nor life, neither angels nor demons, neither our fears for today nor our worries about tomorrow—not even the powers of hell can separate us from God's love. No power in the sky above or in the earth below—indeed, nothing in all creation will ever be able to separate us from the love of God that is revealed in Christ Jesus our Lord.

ROMANS 8:38–39 NLT

I'd be lost without this promise, Lord. Thank You for Your unstoppable love!

ANSWERS TO PRAYER

PRAYER REQUESTS

PRAISES

Monday, May 3

In him our hearts rejoice, for we trust in his holy name. May your unfailing love be with us, LORD, *even as we put our hope in you.*

PSALM 33:21–22 NIV

Lord, I trust in Your holy name, and that gives me every reason to rejoice. Help me spread Your joy. Though I never want to ignore or deny the fact that there is real pain, sorrow, and suffering in this life, I want to show others that even during all that, there is reason to rejoice. We can rest in Your unfailing love and trustworthy promises.

PRAYER REQUESTS

PRAISES

ANSWERS TO PRAYER

Tuesday, May 4

Cast all your anxiety on him because he cares for you. Be alert and of sober mind. Your enemy the devil prowls around like a roaring lion looking for someone to devour. Resist him, standing firm in the faith.

1 PETER 5:7–9 NIV

Lord, thank You that I can throw all my worries at You. Destroy them like only You can, and fill me with Your peace. You are always greater than the enemy, and with Your help and protection, I will stand strong and resist him.

ANSWERS TO PRAYER

PRAYER REQUESTS

PRAISES

Wednesday, May 5

May the God who gives endurance and encouragement give you the same attitude of mind toward each other that Christ Jesus had, so that with one mind and one voice you may glorify the God and Father of our Lord Jesus Christ.

ROMANS 15:5–6 NIV

Endurance and encouragement are the key things I need to patiently wait on You, Lord. Please keep those coming in my life. Thank You!

PRAYER REQUESTS

ANSWERS TO PRAYER

PRAISES

Thursday, May 6

NATIONAL DAY OF PRAYER

One day Jesus told his disciples a story to show that they should always pray and never give up.
Luke 18:1 NLT

Dear Jesus, it's such a blessing to know that You always want us to keep praying to You and never give up. Thank You for sharing Your parables to teach us. Keep me coming back constantly to the goodness of Your Word and to meeting with You in prayer.

ANSWERS TO PRAYER

PRAYER REQUESTS

PRAISES

Friday, May 7

Let us hold fast the confession of our hope without wavering, for he who promised is faithful. And let us consider how to stir up one another to love and good works, not neglecting to meet together, as is the habit of some, but encouraging one another, and all the more as you see the Day drawing near.
HEBREWS 10:23–25 ESV

My hope is secure in You, Lord. Help me and all those who love You constantly encourage and motivate one another to be faithful to You—because You are faithful to us!

PRAYER REQUESTS

ANSWERS TO PRAYER

PRAISES

Saturday, May 8

Keep your lives free from the love of money and be content with what you have, because God has said, "Never will I leave you; never will I forsake you."
HEBREWS 13:5 NIV

Lord, make me smart regarding money. Help me not to spend too much, and help me not to focus on always having more. I want to be satisfied and confident with what You bless me with. Give me wisdom, self-control, and generosity. Remind me that what makes me truly rich is that You are my Lord and Savior.

ANSWERS TO PRAYER

PRAYER REQUESTS

PRAISES

Sunday, May 9

MOTHER'S DAY

Love is patient and kind. Love is not jealous or boastful or proud or rude. It does not demand its own way. It is not irritable, and it keeps no record of being wronged. It does not rejoice about injustice but rejoices whenever the truth wins out. Love never gives up, never loses faith, is always hopeful, and endures through every circumstance.

1 Corinthians 13:4–7 NLT

Lord, thank You for the mothers in the world who love imperfectly—yet so close to the way this passage describes. Have mercy on those who have never felt the love of a mother like this. Above all, remind us that You are the source of all genuine love.

PRAYER REQUESTS

ANSWERS TO PRAYER

PRAISES

Monday, May 10

But let all who take refuge in you rejoice; let them sing joyful praises forever. Spread your protection over them, that all who love your name may be filled with joy. For you bless the godly, O LORD; you surround them with your shield of love.

PSALM 5:11–12 NLT

My refuge is in You, Lord, and I love Your great name. Thank You for surrounding and protecting me with Your love and care. I praise You and sing with joy because You are my safe place and my Savior!

ANSWERS TO PRAYER

PRAYER REQUESTS

PRAISES

Tuesday, May 11

Give your burdens to the LORD and he will take care of you. He will not permit the godly to slip and fall.
PSALM 55:22 NLT

Thank You for wanting to take my burdens and anxieties away from me, Lord! Remind me to give them to You. I trust You to take good care of me, protect me, and fill me with peace.

PRAYER REQUESTS

ANSWERS TO PRAYER

PRAISES

Wednesday, May 12

Love is patient and kind. Love is not jealous or boastful or proud or rude. It does not demand its own way. It is not irritable, and it keeps no record of being wronged.

1 Corinthians 13:4–5 NLT

You know the situation that's testing my patience and kindness right now, Lord. I sure need Your help to extend grace, love, and forgiveness. I want to depend on You completely as I navigate this conflict.

PRAYER REQUESTS

ANSWERS TO PRAYER

PRAISES

Thursday, May 13

"For I hold you by your right hand—I, the Lord *your God. And I say to you, 'Don't be afraid. I am here to help you.'"*
Isaiah 41:13 NLT

What an amazing blessing it is to focus on You holding my right hand, God! Remind me every moment that Your goodness and power are right here with me through Your Holy Spirit. Show me who I need to share this truth with today.

PRAYER REQUESTS

ANSWERS TO PRAYER

PRAISES

Friday, May 14

Turn from evil and do good; then you will dwell in the land forever. For the Lord loves the just and will not forsake his faithful ones. Wrongdoers will be completely destroyed; the offspring of the wicked will perish. The righteous will inherit the land and dwell in it forever.

PSALM 37:27–29 NIV

Lord, remind me that You will never forsake Your faithful ones. Help me to trust that You have ultimate control over wickedness and evil. Help me focus on faithfully following You and Your Word.

ANSWERS TO PRAYER

PRAYER REQUESTS

PRAISES

Saturday, May 15

Dear friends, never take revenge. Leave that to the righteous anger of God. For the Scriptures say, "I will take revenge; I will pay them back," says the LORD. Instead, "If your enemies are hungry, feed them. If they are thirsty, give them something to drink. In doing this, you will heap burning coals of shame on their heads." Don't let evil conquer you, but conquer evil by doing good.

ROMANS 12:19–21 NLT

Lord, give me the right gentleness, kindness, and self-control to follow Your commands and let *You* serve justice.

PRAYER REQUESTS

ANSWERS TO PRAYER

PRAISES

Sunday, May 16

Most important of all, continue to show deep love for each other, for love covers a multitude of sins. Cheerfully share your home with those who need a meal or a place to stay. God has given each of you a gift from his great variety of spiritual gifts. Use them well to serve one another.

1 PETER 4:8–10 NLT

Lord, help me see the gifts You've given me. Then help me love people in practical, tangible ways as I use my gifts to bless and encourage others—for Your glory and to help grow Your kingdom.

ANSWERS TO PRAYER

PRAYER REQUESTS

PRAISES

Monday, May 17

Dear brothers and sisters, I close my letter with these last words: Be joyful. Grow to maturity. Encourage each other. Live in harmony and peace. Then the God of love and peace will be with you.

2 Corinthians 13:11 NLT

Lord, thank You for these straightforward, practical tips from Paul in Your Word. Help me not to complicate and overthink things as I follow You. Help me to simply choose joy, keep growing in wisdom and knowledge of You, encourage others, and live in harmony and peace.

PRAYER REQUESTS

ANSWERS TO PRAYER

PRAISES

Tuesday, May 18

Those who are dominated by the sinful nature think about sinful things, but those who are controlled by the Holy Spirit think about things that please the Spirit. So letting your sinful nature control your mind leads to death. But letting the Spirit control your mind leads to life and peace.

ROMANS 8:5–6 NLT

Fill my mind with Your Holy Spirit, Lord. I want to be controlled completely by You and experience true life and peace.

PRAYER REQUESTS

ANSWERS TO PRAYER

PRAISES

Wednesday, May 19

In his kindness God called you to share in his eternal glory by means of Christ Jesus. So after you have suffered a little while, he will restore, support, and strengthen you, and he will place you on a firm foundation. All power to him forever! Amen.

1 Peter 5:10–11 NLT

Lord, when I'm struggling, help me remember that no suffering will last forever. You are good and kind and full of mercy. You will help me through every trial and bring me to victory on the other side of it.

PRAYER REQUESTS

PRAISES

ANSWERS TO PRAYER

Thursday, May 20

Then God looked over all he had made, and he saw that it was very good!
GENESIS 1:31 NLT

Dear God, yes—Your creation *is* very good! I'm amazed by the beauty and magnificence of the natural world around me. Thank You for creating such a glorious world to live in. And thank You for creating me and all people in Your image. We love beauty, and we love to create because You designed us that way. I praise You!

ANSWERS TO PRAYER

PRAYER REQUESTS

PRAISES

Friday, May 21

She speaks with wisdom, and faithful instruction is on her tongue.
PROVERBS 31:26 NIV

Lord, please let this be true of me. Fill me with Your wisdom and faithful instruction. Then help me share it with others, especially among my close family and friends, and in any other ways You ask me to. Let me be someone others look up to because I look first and foremost to You.

PRAYER REQUESTS

ANSWERS TO PRAYER

PRAISES

Saturday, May 22

The acts of the flesh are obvious: sexual immorality, impurity and debauchery; idolatry and witchcraft; hatred, discord, jealousy, fits of rage, selfish ambition, dissensions, factions and envy; drunkenness, orgies, and the like. I warn you, as I did before, that those who live like this will not inherit the kingdom of God.

GALATIANS 5:19–21 NIV

Lord, help me and those I love to have good self-control so we can avoid all these things. For those already caught up in them, help me shine Your light so they can see that You are the way out of sin's darkness.

ANSWERS TO PRAYER

PRAYER REQUESTS

PRAISES

Sunday, May 23

Be on guard. Stand firm in the faith. Be courageous.
Be strong. And do everything with love.
1 Corinthians 16:13–14 NLT

Lord, don't let me forget that the enemy wants to pull me away from faith in You and destroy me. Please give me wisdom, protection, courage, and especially love as I firmly depend on You.

PRAYER REQUESTS

ANSWERS TO PRAYER

PRAISES

Monday, May 24

Joyful are people of integrity, who follow the instructions of the LORD.
Joyful are those who obey his laws and search for him with all their hearts.

PSALM 119:1–2 NLT

Lord, keep me coming back regularly to all of Psalm 119 to read and be refreshed. I love Your Word that teaches me, guides me, protects me, and brings me great joy!

ANSWERS TO PRAYER

PRAYER REQUESTS

PRAISES

Tuesday, May 25

Deceit is in the hearts of those who plot evil,
but those who promote peace have joy.
PROVERBS 12:20 NIV

Deceit, lies, evil, strife, violence, destruction and the like are all things I want no part of. On the other hand, truth, peace, and joy go hand in hand and come from You. Remind me of that every day, Lord. Keep me following Your good commands that lead to blessing.

PRAYER REQUESTS

ANSWERS TO PRAYER

PRAISES

Wednesday, May 26

Preach the word; be prepared in season and out of season; correct,
rebuke and encourage—with great patience and careful instruction.
For the time will come when people will not put up with sound doctrine.
Instead, to suit their own desires, they will gather around them a
great number of teachers to say what their itching ears want to hear.
They will turn their ears away from the truth and turn aside to myths.
2 TIMOTHY 4:2–4 NIV

Lord, keep bringing me back to this Scripture to remind me how important it is to know Your Word, live out Your Word, and patiently share and teach Your Word.

ANSWERS TO PRAYER

PRAYER REQUESTS

PRAISES

Thursday, May 27

Now all glory to God, who is able, through his mighty power at work within us, to accomplish infinitely more than we might ask or think. Glory to him in the church and in Christ Jesus through all generations forever and ever! Amen.

Ephesians 3:20–21 NLT

Father God, I've seen Your goodness in my life and in the lives of my loved ones already, and it's amazing to ponder that You can go infinitely beyond what we ask or imagine. Thank You in advance for your blessings. You're incredible, God!

PRAYER REQUESTS

ANSWERS TO PRAYER

PRAISES

Friday, May 28

For we live by faith, not by sight.
2 CORINTHIANS 5:7 NIV

When I feel discouraged, Lord, remind me of this truth and keep me committed to You. It's okay if I can't *see* what You're doing in the literal sense of the word. I live by faith in You, and You are worthy! Your promises are true, and I trust You. Show me who else needs this encouragement—to live by faith in You and not by sight—and help me share it with them.

ANSWERS TO PRAYER

PRAYER REQUESTS

PRAISES

Saturday, May 29

Don't live like fools, but like those who are wise. Make the most of every opportunity in these evil days. Don't act thoughtlessly, but understand what the Lord wants you to do. Don't be drunk with wine, because that will ruin your life. Instead, be filled with the Holy Spirit, singing psalms and hymns and spiritual songs among yourselves, and making music to the Lord in your hearts. And give thanks for everything to God the Father in the name of our Lord Jesus Christ.

EPHESIANS 5:15–20 NLT

Lord, I want to be careful, wise, and controlled in how I live, in the ways Your Word instructs.

PRAYER REQUESTS

PRAISES

ANSWERS TO PRAYER

Sunday, May 30

For God so loved the world that he gave his one and only Son, that whoever believes in him shall not perish but have eternal life. For God did not send his Son into the world to condemn the world, but to save the world through him.

John 3:16–17 NIV

Father God, I praise You for the ways You *so love* us! I never want the truth of this passage to be far from my mind so that I can share it widely—and help lead more people into a saving relationship with Your Son, our one and only risen Savior.

ANSWERS TO PRAYER

PRAYER REQUESTS

PRAISES

Monday, May 31

MEMORIAL DAY

Make a joyful noise to the LORD, all the earth! Serve the LORD with gladness! Come into his presence with singing! . . . For the LORD is good; his steadfast love endures forever, and his faithfulness to all generations.

PSALM 100:1–2, 5 ESV

I sing with joy to You today, Lord; You are worthy of all praise! If I ever forget the joy I find in you, remind me to turn up the music and sing once again.

PRAYER REQUESTS

ANSWERS TO PRAYER

PRAISES

JUNE 2027

Hope will never fail to satisfy our deepest need because the Holy Spirit that was given to us has flooded our hearts with God's love.
ROMANS 5:5 VOICE

SUNDAY	MONDAY	TUESDAY	WEDNESDAY	THURSDAY	FRIDAY	SATURDAY
		1	2	3	4	5
6	7	8	9	10	11	12
13	14 Flag Day	15	16	17	18	19 Juneteenth
20 Father's Day	21 First Day of Summer	22	23	24	25	26
27	28	29	30			

Warmer weather, more sunlight, fun plans, and vacations do much to lift the spirit, but they pale in comparison with the eternal hope and joy we have in Jesus. Ask the Holy Spirit to flood your heart with God's love, and be transformed from the inside out!

Tuesday, June 1

"See, God has come to save me. I will trust in him and not be afraid. The LORD GOD is my strength and my song; he has given me victory."
ISAIAH 12:2 NLT

I will not fear the future, Lord, because You are with me. You are my Savior for today and for eternity, and I trust You to take care of me. Remind me of Your past victories in my life, and give me the courage to know that You and I will win over every challenge and every obstacle.

PRAYER REQUESTS

ANSWERS TO PRAYER

PRAISES

Wednesday, June 2

What else does the Eternal ask of you but to live justly and to love kindness and to walk with your True God in all humility?

MICAH 6:8 VOICE

I know of so many unfair, heartbreaking situations, Lord—people who need You to step in and let Your justice flow. But your timing isn't the same as what I might want. While we wait for You to make everything right, I will work toward living a just life and show kindness to others in Your name.

ANSWERS TO PRAYER

PRAYER REQUESTS

PRAISES

Thursday, June 3

You are good and do only good; teach me your decrees.
PSALM 119:68 NLT

I never have to wonder if Your motives are good, Lord—because You are *only* good! Your plan is perfect; Your love is authentic and everlasting. Your grace covers all my sins, and Your wisdom gives me life! Help me know and love Your Word more as I read and study scripture. Give me discernment to understand what I'm reading so I can apply it to my life.

PRAYER REQUESTS

PRAISES

ANSWERS TO PRAYER

Friday, June 4

"I am the LORD, and I do not change."
MALACHI 3:6 NLT

Things change around me so quickly that it's hard to keep up, Father. The news cycle, scientific discoveries, technology, world events, politics, the economy. Even my own relationships, health, and situations—it's all too much to take in! But when everything else in my life is in flux, You are my anchor in that storm of change because You *do not change.* I trust You in all things at all times. Thank You!

ANSWERS TO PRAYER

PRAYER REQUESTS

PRAISES

Saturday, June 5

Those who let their sinful old selves tell them what to do live under that power of their sinful old selves. But those who let the Holy Spirit tell them what to do are under His power. If your sinful old self is the boss over your mind, it leads to death. But if the Holy Spirit is the boss over your mind, it leads to life and peace.

ROMANS 8:5–6 NLV

Holy Spirit, please move in my heart and cover me with abundant life and peace.

PRAYER REQUESTS

PRAISES

ANSWERS TO PRAYER

Sunday, June 6

Dear friends, let us love each other, because love comes from God. Those who love are God's children and they know God.
1 John 4:7 NLV

Father, remind me that the best way to bring others to Christ is to love them like You love me—unconditionally and unreservedly. Thank You for lavishing Your love on me throughout my life. Let Your love prompt me to think of others, serve others, and give You all the glory in the process.

ANSWERS TO PRAYER

PRAYER REQUESTS

PRAISES

Monday, June 7

My lips will call out for joy when I sing praises to You. You have set my soul free.

Psalm 71:23 NLV

I am not a slave to my former self, my old insecurities, my anxiety of the past. When I realize this truth and I cling to You, Lord, I can begin to experience true freedom! I will worship You gladly, Father, because You are worthy of every syllable I can utter to lift You higher!

PRAYER REQUESTS

ANSWERS TO PRAYER

PRAISES

Tuesday, June 8

But the wisdom that comes from heaven is first of all pure. Then it gives peace. It is gentle and willing to obey. It is full of loving-kindness and of doing good. It has no doubts and does not pretend to be something it is not.

James 3:17 NLV

God, as I grow deeper in my faith and relationship with You, Your peace motivates me to be more like You: humbler, more genuine, more trusting, and more sure-footed. With You, I have everything I need!

ANSWERS TO PRAYER

PRAYER REQUESTS

PRAISES

Wednesday, June 9

This is my last gift to you, this example of a way of life: a life of hard work, a life of helping the weak, a life that echoes every day those words of Jesus our King, who said, "It is more blessed to give than to receive."
Acts 20:35 voice

The more I serve others, Father, the more I realize these are the things that are truly fulfilling. Give me the strength to always work hard and help others in Your name and for Your glory.

PRAYER REQUESTS

ANSWERS TO PRAYER

PRAISES

Thursday, June 10

Whenever we have the opportunity, we should do good to everyone—especially to those in the family of faith.
GALATIANS 6:10 NLT

I come today, Holy Spirit, asking for obvious, specific ways I can do good in Your name. Prick my conscience, and nudge me in the right direction. Do whatever You need to do to wake me up to the people around me who need help, encouragement, and blessing.

PRAYER REQUESTS

ANSWERS TO PRAYER

PRAISES

Friday, June 11

Faith comes from hearing the message, and the message
is heard through the word about Christ.
ROMANS 10:17 NIV

Thank You, God, for the people You put in my life who first shared Your love with me. I don't take for granted the fact that I know of Jesus' life, death, and resurrection—and that through hearing the gospel and accepting His salvation, my faith is alive in You! Show me who You want me to share this life-changing message with today.

PRAYER REQUESTS

PRAISES

ANSWERS TO PRAYER

Saturday, June 12

Don't fight against the one who is working evil against you. If someone strikes you on the right cheek, you are to turn and offer him your left cheek.
Matthew 5:39 VOICE

When I feel personally attacked, ridiculed, persecuted, or taken advantage of, Lord, I admit that I want to stick up for myself and strike back. But You call me to live a life of love and faith. I know Your justice will prevail. Today I am holding on to that promise, Father!

ANSWERS TO PRAYER

PRAYER REQUESTS

PRAISES

Sunday, June 13

I pray that you will know the love of Christ. His love goes beyond anything we can understand. I pray that you will be filled with God Himself.

Ephesians 3:19 NLV

Your Word has so much to say about Your love, Lord, yet it is still so mysterious to me. Your love never gives up on me, no matter how many times I falter. Your love for me stands strong even when my faith wavers. Your love is the thing that sustains me every day.

PRAYER REQUESTS

ANSWERS TO PRAYER

PRAISES

Monday, June 14

FLAG DAY

"There is rejoicing in the presence of the angels of God over one sinner who repents."

LUKE 15:10 NIV

Lord, today I'm praying for someone in my life who needs You. They seem so far from You right now, but I know that no one is beyond hope, beyond Your reach. Your love is the thing that can change everything for them. I will continue to pray, continue to ask You to move in their heart, because I know You love them even more than I do.

ANSWERS TO PRAYER

PRAYER REQUESTS

PRAISES

Tuesday, June 15

Join us, and pursue a life that creates peace and builds up our brothers and sisters.
Romans 14:19 voice

Father, please grow my church to become a haven of peace in this chaotic world. Let us be a group of people who are united in our love for Jesus and who encourage one another in all ways at all times. We want to be a community that shares life with one another—both the good and the hard things—and welcomes new believers with open arms.

PRAYER REQUESTS

ANSWERS TO PRAYER

PRAISES

Wednesday, June 16

Whoever pursues righteousness and kindness will find life, righteousness, and honor.
PROVERBS 21:21 ESV

Lord, there's so much going on in my life. Some days I feel like all I can do is keep my head above water. But You have so much more for me. Give me the strength to pursue the important, lasting goodness You have for me. I am listening, Lord. Tell me what You want me to do.

ANSWERS TO PRAYER

PRAYER REQUESTS

PRAISES

Thursday, June 17

The Lord is good, a safe place in times of trouble. And He knows those who come to Him to be safe.
NAHUM 1:7 NLV

Father, too often I wrongly think I must rely only on myself—that I must be strong enough to withstand a storm of troubles without help. But Your arms are strong to hold me close, and Your heart listens when I cry out to You. So I will run to You, knowing You are my good, safe place.

PRAYER REQUESTS

PRAISES

ANSWERS TO PRAYER

Friday, June 18

He took on our sins in His body when He died on the cross
so that we, being dead to sin, can live for righteousness.
1 Peter 2:24 VOICE

It's impossible to imagine the physical, mental, and spiritual weight of humanity's sins while You were on the cross, Jesus. How did You withstand it—the betrayal, the darkness, the evil of all that sin? Yet even in the middle of that heart-wrenching anguish, You remained committed to God's plan. You ushered in salvation with Your faithfulness. Hallelujah!

ANSWERS TO PRAYER

PRAYER REQUESTS

PRAISES

Saturday, June 19

JUNETEENTH

Do not let sin control the way you live; do not give in to sinful desires.
ROMANS 6:12 NLT

I want You to take back control of my life from sin, Father. I give it all to You. I know this is something I'll need to do again and again because I am anything but perfect. Thank You for Your perfect love, perfect forgiveness, and the perfect way You help me—little by little—to become more like You.

PRAYER REQUESTS

ANSWERS TO PRAYER

PRAISES

Sunday, June 20

FATHER'S DAY

Consider the kind of extravagant love the Father has lavished on us—
He calls us children of God! It's true; we are His beloved children.
1 John 3:1 voice

I'm celebrating fathers today, Lord, and I'm thankful for the influence they have in my life—dads, grandfathers, uncles, and spiritual fathers alike. Please bless and shower your goodness on them today and every day! Thank You for being the example of the perfect Father for Your children.

ANSWERS TO PRAYER

PRAYER REQUESTS

PRAISES

Monday, June 21

FIRST DAY OF SUMMER

The Eternal your God is standing right here among you,
and He is the champion who will rescue you. He will
joyfully celebrate over you; He will rest in His love for you;
He will joyfully sing because of you like a new husband.
ZEPHANIAH 3:17 VOICE

You delight in the victories of Your children, Lord! Today I'm asking for a win that we can celebrate together—because there's no party I want to attend more.

PRAYER REQUESTS

ANSWERS TO PRAYER

PRAISES

Tuesday, June 22

Kindness, peace, love—may they never stop blooming in you and from you.
JUDE 1:2 VOICE

Lord, make my heart a fertile plot of soil where all Your beauty can blossom and thrive. With help from the Holy Spirit, I will harvest kindness, peace, and love—enough to share with everyone around me! May my life be a beautiful-smelling bouquet full of color that honors You.

ANSWERS TO PRAYER

PRAYER REQUESTS

PRAISES

Wednesday, June 23

We should help others do what is right and build them up in the Lord.
Romans 15:2 NLT

Father, help me be a godly encouragement to the people in my life—not in a judgmental way, but in an authentically loving way. When we build our lives on Your truth, Your Word, Your wisdom, that's when we can withstand the daily difficulties and the big trials in this life—together.

PRAYER REQUESTS

PRAISES

ANSWERS TO PRAYER

Thursday, June 24

Every good gift bestowed, every perfect gift received comes to us from above, courtesy of the Father of lights. He is consistent. He won't change His mind or play tricks in the shadows.

James 1:17 voice

There are many things in my life, Lord, that aren't consistent, and I may have to guess about motive behind an action. But You are the definition of *consistent*. I praise You because You do not change Your mind. You do not manipulate. You are true and loyal and upright in all Your ways.

ANSWERS TO PRAYER

PRAYER REQUESTS

PRAISES

Friday, June 25

I am sure that God Who began the good work in you will keep on working in you until the day Jesus Christ comes again.
PHILIPPIANS 1:6 NLV

I am Your work in progress, God. Thank You for beginning that good work and claiming me as Your child when I professed Jesus as the Lord of my life. You're remaking me from the inside out, and I'm not the same person I was before I knew You. Thank You for never giving up on me, no matter what!

PRAYER REQUESTS

ANSWERS TO PRAYER

PRAISES

Saturday, June 26

Human anger is a futile exercise that will never produce God's kind of justice in this world.
JAMES 1:20 VOICE

I want so badly to change things, Lord. I'm so frustrated with the state of the world that sometimes it makes me want to scream! But an outburst into the void accomplishes nothing, and James 1:20 reminds me that getting angry does not bring about Your justice. So instead, I will bring my concerns to You and lay them at Your feet, trusting You and Your will.

ANSWERS TO PRAYER

PRAYER REQUESTS

PRAISES

Sunday, June 27

Does love hurt anyone? Absolutely not.
In fact, love achieves everything the law requires.
Romans 13:10 voice

Today I will welcome and embrace Your perfect love, God! Because when I actively receive Your love and willingly share it with everyone, I know You can heal the brokenness I feel and see all around me. I want Your love to be a soothing balm that comforts, encourages, and restores my heart and the hearts of others.

PRAYER REQUESTS

PRAISES

ANSWERS TO PRAYER

Monday, June 28

Let us keep looking to Jesus. Our faith comes from Him and He is the One Who makes it perfect. He did not give up when He had to suffer shame and die on a cross. He knew of the joy that would be His later. Now He is sitting at the right side of God.

HEBREWS 12:2 NLV

Jesus, You are the master of delayed gratification. Help me to always keep eternity in mind and do the things that bring You joy and glorify the Father.

ANSWERS TO PRAYER

PRAYER REQUESTS

PRAISES

Tuesday, June 29

The God of peace will soon crush Satan under your feet.
ROMANS 16:20 NLT

Some days I feel attacked on every side, Lord. On those days, I will cling to the promise found in Romans 16:20. With Your help and by Your strength, we are defeating the powers of darkness! Satan has no room here with his tricks and temptations and lies. Instead, Your peace offers me authenticity and truth—two things I desperately need.

PRAYER REQUESTS

PRAISES

ANSWERS TO PRAYER

Wednesday, June 30

"Give to those who ask, and don't turn away from those who want to borrow."
MATTHEW 5:42 NLT

God, You are the good Creator, and the Bible tells me that You own everything. Even my paycheck belongs to You. Teach me how to live wisely with the blessings You give me—to live a generous life that's willing to take care of others' needs when I can and when You call me to help.

ANSWERS TO PRAYER

PRAYER REQUESTS

PRAISES

JULY 2027

Let the whole earth sing to the LORD!
Each day proclaim the good news that he saves.
1 CHRONICLES 16:23 NLT

SUNDAY	MONDAY	TUESDAY	WEDNESDAY	THURSDAY	FRIDAY	SATURDAY
				1	2	3
4 Independence Day	5	6	7	8	9	10
11	12	13	14	15	16	17
18	19	20	21	22	23	24
25	26	27	28	29	30	31

What a blessing to celebrate freedom to live and think and speak our minds the way we want to. As Christians, above all else, let's use our independence to share the good news that only Jesus saves people from their sin. Let's proclaim Him as much as we can—openly, sincerely, joyfully, *daily*!

Thursday, July 1

As Jesus was starting out on his way to Jerusalem, a man came running up to him, knelt down, and asked, "Good Teacher, what must I do to inherit eternal life?" "Why do you call me good?" Jesus asked. "Only God is truly good."

MARK 10:17–18 NLT

Jesus, in this passage You were emphasizing that You *are* God and the perfect example of what "good" means. Thank You! Help me follow and obey You always, the best I possibly can!

ANSWERS TO PRAYER

PRAYER REQUESTS

PRAISES

Friday, July 2

You desired faithfulness even in the womb;
you taught me wisdom in that secret place.
Psalm 51:6 niv

Lord, You designed me in my mother's womb, and even from there You were creating me to want to know and love You faithfully—and to need and receive Your wonderful grace. I pray that more people would realize how You created all human beings, and that you have purpose for us from the first moment of life in our mothers' wombs. We are all formed in Your image with priceless value, and that's incredible!

PRAYER REQUESTS

ANSWERS TO PRAYER

PRAISES

Saturday, July 3

He said to them, "Let the children come to me. Don't stop them! For the Kingdom of God belongs to those who are like these children.
15 I tell you the truth, anyone who doesn't receive the Kingdom of God like a child will never enter it." Then he took the children in his arms and placed his hands on their heads and blessed them.

Mark 10:14–16 NLT

Lord, thank You for showing the example of honoring children. Help me always have the gentleness and love for them that You do.

PRAYER REQUESTS

ANSWERS TO PRAYER

PRAISES

Sunday, July 4

INDEPENDENCE DAY

You, my brothers and sisters, were called to be free. But do not use your freedom to indulge the flesh; rather, serve one another humbly in love. For the entire law is fulfilled in keeping this one command: "Love your neighbor as yourself."

GALATIANS 5:13–14 NIV

Dear Lord, what a beautiful thing it is to be free in You because of Your grace and mercy! Please help me never let it go to my head. Keep my heart soft and my mind full of Your wisdom. Keep me humble and helpful to others as I point them to You and serve them in kindness, truth, and love.

PRAYER REQUESTS

PRAISES

ANSWERS TO PRAYER

Monday, July 5

Unless the Lord *had helped me, I would soon have settled in the silence of the grave. I cried out, "I am slipping!" but your unfailing love, O* Lord *supported me. When doubts filled my mind, your comfort gave me renewed hope and cheer.*

Psalm 94:17–19 NLT

Doubts do fill my mind sometimes, Lord. I can't deny that. You know my mind and heart and every thought I think. Whenever I start to slip toward doubt and discouragement, pull me back close to renew my confidence, hope, and joy in You.

ANSWERS TO PRAYER

PRAYER REQUESTS

PRAISES

Tuesday, July 6

Hear me as I pray, O Lord. Be merciful and answer me! My heart has heard you say, "Come and talk with me." And my heart responds, "Lord, I am coming." Do not turn your back on me. Do not reject your servant in anger. You have always been my helper. Don't leave me now; don't abandon me, O God of my salvation! Even if my father and mother abandon me, the Lord will hold me close.

Psalm 27:7–10 NLT

Because You will always keep me close, I have nothing to fear. I can have perfect peace. Thank You, Lord!

PRAYER REQUESTS

PRAISES

ANSWERS TO PRAYER

Wednesday, July 7

Then the Lord *said to me, "Write my answer plainly on tablets, so that a runner can carry the correct message to others. This vision is for a future time. It describes the end, and it will be fulfilled. If it seems slow in coming, wait patiently, for it will surely take place. It will not be delayed."*

Habakkuk 2:2–3 NLT

Lord, You heard and answered Habakkuk, and I know You hear and answer Your people today. Help me wait patiently for You, even when Your answers aren't coming in the timeline I prefer.

ANSWERS TO PRAYER

PRAYER REQUESTS

PRAISES

Thursday, July 8

Give thanks to the LORD, for he is good! His faithful love endures forever. Has the LORD redeemed you? Then speak out! Tell others he has redeemed you from your enemies. For he has gathered the exiles from many lands, from east and west, from north and south.

PSALM 107:1–3 NLT

Lord, I want to speak out wide and far about Your goodness, Your faithfulness, and Your great love! Make me bold for You, with Your truth and compassion flowing from me.

PRAYER REQUESTS

ANSWERS TO PRAYER

PRAISES

Friday, July 9

"His master replied, 'Well done, good and faithful servant! You have been faithful with a few things; I will put you in charge of many things. Come and share your master's happiness!'"
MATTHEW 25:21 NIV

Lord, I long to hear You say these words to me one day in heaven. I want to honor You with everything I do in life. Thank You for Your grace that covers my mistakes. Help me faithfully follow and serve You.

ANSWERS TO PRAYER

PRAYER REQUESTS

PRAISES

Saturday, July 10

For the Lord God is our sun and our shield. He gives us grace and glory. The Lord will withhold no good thing from those who do what is right. O Lord of Heaven's Armies, what joy for those who trust in you.

Psalm 84:11–12 NLT

My sun and shield, Lord—what a beautiful way to think of You. Let me focus daily on the truth of how You love me and give me every good thing I need, plus true joy both now and forever. Thank You!

PRAYER REQUESTS

ANSWERS TO PRAYER

PRAISES

Sunday, July 11

Put on then, as God's chosen ones, holy and beloved, compassionate hearts, kindness, humility, meekness, and patience, bearing with one another and, if one has a complaint against another, forgiving each other; as the Lord has forgiven you, so you also must forgive. And above all these put on love, which binds everything together in perfect harmony. And let the peace of Christ rule in your hearts, to which indeed you were called in one body. And be thankful.

COLOSSIANS 3:12–15 ESV

Lord, keep me coming back to Your good instructions on how to show real love to others.

ANSWERS TO PRAYER

PRAYER REQUESTS

PRAISES

Monday, July 12

And behold, the star that they had seen when it rose went before them until it came to rest over the place where the child was. When they saw the star, they rejoiced exceedingly with great joy.
MATTHEW 2:9–10 ESV

People are searching for You, Jesus. And when they find You, they find real joy. Help me be a shining light, leading others to You.

PRAYER REQUESTS

ANSWERS TO PRAYER

PRAISES

Tuesday, July 13

"Though the mountains be shaken and the hills be removed, yet my unfailing love for you will not be shaken nor my covenant of peace be removed," says the Lord*, who has compassion on you.*

Isaiah 54:10 NIV

Total chaos can go on all around me, but You still give me peace, Lord. I trust in Your unfailing love and promises.

PRAYER REQUESTS

ANSWERS TO PRAYER

PRAISES

Wednesday, July 14

But do not overlook this one fact, beloved, that with the Lord one day is as a thousand years, and a thousand years as one day. The Lord is not slow to fulfill his promise as some count slowness, but is patient toward you, not wishing that any should perish, but that all should reach repentance.
2 PETER 3:8–9 ESV

Thank You for Your great patience and love for all people, Lord.

PRAYER REQUESTS

ANSWERS TO PRAYER

PRAISES

Thursday, July 15

The LORD is good, a strong refuge when trouble comes. He is close to those who trust in him. But he will sweep away his enemies in an overwhelming flood. He will pursue his foes into the darkness of night.
NAHUM 1:7–8 NLT

You are so good, Lord, and You are the only one who serves perfect justice. Thank You for being a strong refuge and close, protective presence for all who trust in You!

PRAYER REQUESTS

ANSWERS TO PRAYER

PRAISES

Friday, July 16

By faith even Sarah, who was past childbearing age, was enabled to bear children because she considered him faithful who had made the promise. And so from this one man, and he as good as dead, came descendants as numerous as the stars in the sky and as countless as the sand on the seashore.

HEBREWS 11:11–12 NIV

Lord, remind me that even when Your promises seem utterly impossible, You are faithful to fulfill them.

PRAYER REQUESTS

ANSWERS TO PRAYER

PRAISES

Saturday, July 17

But you, Timothy, are a man of God; so run from all these evil things. Pursue righteousness and a godly life, along with faith, love, perseverance, and gentleness. Fight the good fight for the true faith. Hold tightly to the eternal life to which God has called you, which you have declared so well before many witnesses.

1 TIMOTHY 6:11–12 NLT

Remind me, Lord, that Paul's good instructions to Timothy are for me to remember daily as well.

ANSWERS TO PRAYER

PRAYER REQUESTS

PRAISES

Sunday, July 18

We can rejoice, too, when we run into problems and trials, for we know that they help us develop endurance. And endurance develops strength of character, and character strengthens our confident hope of salvation. And this hope will not lead to disappointment. For we know how dearly God loves us, because he has given us the Holy Spirit to fill our hearts with his love.
Romans 5:3–5 NLT

Lord, Your great love is what gets me through any problem and trial. Thank You for the presence of Your Holy Spirit helping me, guiding me, carrying me.

PRAYER REQUESTS

ANSWERS TO PRAYER

PRAISES

Monday, July 19

Trust in the LORD and do good. Then you will live safely in the land and prosper. Take delight in the LORD, and he will give you your heart's desires. Commit everything you do to the LORD. Trust him, and he will help you. He will make your innocence radiate like the dawn, and the justice of your cause will shine like the noonday sun.

PSALM 37:3–6 NLT

It's so cool how You multiply joy, Lord. When I delight in You, You just keep adding blessing upon blessing. Thank You!

ANSWERS TO PRAYER

PRAYER REQUESTS

PRAISES

Tuesday, July 20

In my distress I prayed to the Lord, *and the* Lord *answered me and set me free. The* Lord *is for me, so I will have no fear. What can mere people do to me? Yes, the* Lord *is for me; he will help me. I will look in triumph at those who hate me. It is better to take refuge in the* Lord *than to trust in people.*

Psalm 118:5–8 NLT

Thank You for the good people in my life, Lord. Above all, I trust in *You* for protection, provision, and peace!

PRAYER REQUESTS

PRAISES

ANSWERS TO PRAYER

Wednesday, July 21

"If you, then, though you are evil, know how to give good gifts to your children, how much more will your Father in heaven give good gifts to those who ask him! So in everything, do to others what you would have them do to you, for this sums up the Law and the Prophets."

MATTHEW 7:11–12 NIV

The only reason any of us knows how to be kind and generous to one another is because You are our loving example, Father. Thank You! Help me to always treat others well, like I want to be treated.

ANSWERS TO PRAYER

PRAYER REQUESTS

PRAISES

Thursday, July 22

"You are the light of the world. . . . Let your light shine before others, that they may see your good deeds and glorify your Father in heaven.

MATTHEW 5:14,16 NIV

Shine through me, Lord. Let my good deeds always glorify You. Forgive me for anything I've done that has shrouded Your love and truth from radiating from me. Help me go forward boldly and brightly for You!

PRAYER REQUESTS

PRAISES

ANSWERS TO PRAYER

Friday, July 23

I listen carefully to what God the LORD is saying, for he speaks peace to his faithful people. But let them not return to their foolish ways. Surely his salvation is near to those who fear him, so our land will be filled with his glory.

PSALM 85:8–9 NLT

Lord, I want to be known as one of Your faithful people. Please bless me with Your peace. Help me stay far from the foolish ways of this world and keep close to You instead.

ANSWERS TO PRAYER

PRAYER REQUESTS

PRAISES

Saturday, July 24

If the godly give in to the wicked, it's like polluting a fountain or muddying a spring. It's not good to eat too much honey, and it's not good to seek honors for yourself. A person without self-control is like a city with broken-down walls.
PROVERBS 25:26–28 NLT

Lord, help me never to give in to the wicked. Help me have self-control over both major and minor things. I want to live a life that is strong and secure, not broken and useless.

PRAYER REQUESTS

PRAISES

ANSWERS TO PRAYER

Sunday, July 25

By our very nature we were subject to God's anger, just like everyone else. But God is so rich in mercy, and he loved us so much, that even though we were dead because of our sins, he gave us life when he raised Christ from the dead. (It is only by God's grace that you have been saved!)

EPHESIANS 2:3–5 NLT

Father God, thank You for loving me so much and making a way through Jesus Christ to give me life instead of death. I'm beyond grateful for Your mercy and grace.

ANSWERS TO PRAYER

PRAYER REQUESTS

PRAISES

Monday, July 26

When the seventy-two disciples returned, they joyfully reported to him, "Lord, even the demons obey us when we use your name!" "Yes," he told them, "I saw Satan fall from heaven like lightning! Look, I have given you authority over all the power of the enemy, and you can walk among snakes and scorpions and crush them. Nothing will injure you. But don't rejoice because evil spirits obey you; rejoice because your names are registered in heaven."

LUKE 10:17–20 NLT

Lord, I have joy because of Your power in my life, and I have even greater joy because my name is registered in heaven. Amazing!

PRAYER REQUESTS

PRAISES

ANSWERS TO PRAYER

Tuesday, July 27

God disciplines us for our good, in order that we may share in his holiness. No discipline seems pleasant at the time, but painful. Later on, however, it produces a harvest of righteousness and peace for those who have been trained by it.
HEBREWS 12:10–11 NIV

Lord, I'm trusting that Your good discipline results in peace. Help me welcome, learn, and grow from it.

PRAYER REQUESTS

ANSWERS TO PRAYER

PRAISES

Wednesday, July 28

"You yourselves know that these hands of mine have supplied my own needs and the needs of my companions. In everything I did, I showed you that by this kind of hard work we must help the weak, remembering the words the Lord Jesus himself said: 'It is more blessed to give than to receive.'"

Acts 20:34–35 NIV

Lord, thank You for Paul's reminder in this passage to show kindness by working hard, taking responsibility, and helping provide for those who can't provide for themselves.

PRAYER REQUESTS

ANSWERS TO PRAYER

PRAISES

Thursday, July 29

Blessed are those you choose and bring near to live in your courts! We are filled with the good things of your house, of your holy temple. You answer us with awesome and righteous deeds, God our Savior. . . . The whole earth is filled with awe at your wonders.

Psalm 65:4–5, 8 NIV

Truly, Lord, I am in awe of You, Your goodness in my life, and Your whole beautiful world!

ANSWERS TO PRAYER

PRAYER REQUESTS

PRAISES

Friday, July 30

Just because they were unfaithful, does that mean God will be unfaithful? Of course not! Even if everyone else is a liar, God is true.
ROMANS 3:3–4 NLT

Father God, You are the one true example of faithfulness. Thank You for being faithful to me, even when I am unfaithful to You, even when I stumble and fall away at times. Forgive me. Help me to always get back up quickly, back to following You, in close fellowship with You.

PRAYER REQUESTS

ANSWERS TO PRAYER

PRAISES

Saturday, July 31

And "don't sin by letting anger control you." Don't let the sun go down while you are still angry, for anger gives a foothold to the devil.
Ephesians 4:26–27 NLT

Lord, keep me in good self-control, never letting anger overtake me. Help me remember it's okay to be angry at things that go against You and Your Word. Give me wisdom and guidance on what to do about them so I don't end up sinning and giving the devil a foothold in my life.

ANSWERS TO PRAYER

PRAYER REQUESTS

PRAISES

AUGUST 2027

"Blessed is the one who trusts in the L*ORD*,
whose confidence is in him."
JEREMIAH 17:7 NIV

SUNDAY	MONDAY	TUESDAY	WEDNESDAY	THURSDAY	FRIDAY	SATURDAY
1	2	3	4	5	6	7
8	9	10	11	12	13	14
15	16	17	18	19	20	21
22	23	24	25	26	27	28
29	30	31				

While the world shouts that self-confidence is the key to success and happiness, God's Word reminds us that we are wisest when our confidence is in Him alone. That means asking about—and then trusting in—His plan. It means waiting on the Lord when the path is unclear. And it means stepping forward in faith when we see Him move.

Sunday, August 1

If you want to be extraordinary—love your enemies! Do good without restraint! Lend with abandon! Don't expect anything in return! Then you'll receive the truly great reward—you will be children of the Most High—for God is kind to the ungrateful and those who are wicked.

Luke 6:35 voice

You created me to be extraordinary, Father, not because of what I can do, but because of what Your Son did on the cross! Help me become less selfish and more selfless—today and every day.

ANSWERS TO PRAYER

PRAYER REQUESTS

PRAISES

Monday, August 2

When my worry is great within me, Your comfort brings joy to my soul.
Psalm 94:19 NLV

I struggle with worry, Lord. . .more often than I want to admit. It's a constant battle to lay down my anxious thoughts and trust You to take care of whatever troubles me. But when I do let go, the peace and comfort that flood in are such a relief! Today I release my grip on my worries and trade it for Your joy.

PRAYER REQUESTS

ANSWERS TO PRAYER

PRAISES

Tuesday, August 3

Since God cares for you, let Him carry all your burdens and worries.
1 Peter 5:7 voice

Of everything I know about You, Father, the fact that You *care* for me is one thing I hold dear to my heart. You *care* when I'm struggling. You *care* when I'm anxious. You *care* when I feel burnt out. Even better than that, You offer to take those struggles and carry them for me—releasing me from what holds me back. Thank You!

ANSWERS TO PRAYER

PRAYER REQUESTS

PRAISES

Wednesday, August 4

Help each other in troubles and problems.
This is the kind of law Christ asks us to obey.
Galatians 6:2 NLV

Jesus, I am so thankful for the connections I have with other Christians. They are truly Your hands and feet in my life. When I need prayer, they are faithful to talk to You about what's going on. When I need encouragement, they build me up. And when I celebrate a win, they love to party with me!

PRAYER REQUESTS

PRAISES

ANSWERS TO PRAYER

Thursday, August 5

We know that God makes all things work together for the good of those who love Him and are chosen to be a part of His plan.
Romans 8:28 NLV

When I'm in the middle of a difficult season, Father, help me remember that someday—maybe soon or maybe years from now—I will see how You are worked *everything* together for my good and Your glory. In the meantime, I will cling to and trust this promise in Romans 8:28.

ANSWERS TO PRAYER

PRAYER REQUESTS

PRAISES

Friday, August 6

You, O Lord, are a God merciful and gracious, slow to anger and abounding in steadfast love and faithfulness.
Psalm 86:15 ESV

Lord, as I grow to be more like You, I realize how far Your mercy stretches over everything You are. Your merciful heart leads to Your gracious kindness to Your children. You are patient with us as we try—and sometimes stumble—to resist temptation and make the right decisions. Your love is faithful and unending, picking us up and dusting us off to try again.

PRAYER REQUESTS

ANSWERS TO PRAYER

PRAISES

Saturday, August 7

So I say, let the Holy Spirit guide your lives. Then you won't be doing what your sinful nature craves. The sinful nature wants to do evil, which is just the opposite of what the Spirit wants. And the Spirit gives us desires that are the opposite of what the sinful nature desires. These two forces are constantly fighting each other, so you are not free to carry out your good intentions.

GALATIANS 5:16–17 NLT

Have Your way with me, Holy Spirit. I want what You want.

ANSWERS TO PRAYER

PRAYER REQUESTS

PRAISES

Sunday, August 8

I am convinced that nothing can ever separate us from God's love. Neither death nor life, neither angels nor demons, neither our fears for today nor our worries about tomorrow— not even the powers of hell can separate us from God's love.
ROMANS 8:38 NLT

Father, Your love is before me, beneath me, beside me, above me, and within me. Today I will go forward with confidence, knowing that nothing will separate me from Your everlasting love.

PRAYER REQUESTS

PRAISES

ANSWERS TO PRAYER

Monday, August 9

Light is spread like seed for those who are right and good, and joy for the pure in heart.
PSALM 97:11 NLV

Create in me a clean heart and a clear purpose to shine Your light in this dark world, Father. I see so many people every day who need hope, who need joy. . .who need *You*. Use me to sow that seed of light, of love. I know You are faithful to cause that seed to sprout and bring new believers to You!

PRAYER REQUESTS

ANSWERS TO PRAYER

PRAISES

Tuesday, August 10

A dry piece of food with peace and quiet is better than a house full of food with fighting.
Proverbs 17:1 NLV

God, I humbly ask You to wrap my family in Your peace. I dearly love the people I'm connected to, but we aren't perfect. Sometimes hurt feelings or unmet expectations lead to conflict—and once a fight starts, it's sometimes hard to stop! Give us wisdom as we try to grow closer to one another and to You.

PRAYER REQUESTS

PRAISES

ANSWERS TO PRAYER

Wednesday, August 11

Live in true devotion to one another, loving each other as sisters and brothers. Be first to honor others by putting them first.
ROMANS 12:10 VOICE

The world has a "me first!" mentality, Lord, and I admit that this wrong attitude often sneaks into my heart. Please let me see others the way You see them, as Your sons and daughters, and my brothers and sisters. Help me remember that when I honor others above myself, You will honor me too.

PRAYER REQUESTS

ANSWERS TO PRAYER

PRAISES

Thursday, August 12

Your overflowing goodness You have kept for those who live in awe of You, and You share Your goodness with those who make You their sanctuary.

PSALM 31:19 VOICE

I praise You, Father, for all that You are. When I take a moment and count the ways I see You working in my life—in big ways and small—I am overcome with gratitude. You provide what I need, and You delight in pouring out Your goodness on me with Your everlasting love and mercy!

PRAYER REQUESTS

ANSWERS TO PRAYER

PRAISES

Friday, August 13

The Word of the Lord is right. He is faithful in all He does.
PSALM 33:4 NLV

Father, when I feel adrift or unsure, lead me to the Bible. Your Word is truth. Your wisdom is sound and will not falter. Your scriptures are living and active and can strengthen my relationship with You by helping me know Your character and Your heart for Your children. Thank You for the blessing of the Bible!

ANSWERS TO PRAYER

PRAYER REQUESTS

PRAISES

Saturday, August 14

Be not quick in your spirit to become angry,
for anger lodges in the heart of fools.
ECCLESIASTES 7:9 ESV

When I'm mad, Lord, I admit that it puts me into a funk. Anger negatively affects the way I view everything and everyone around me, and it's not honoring to You. Buoy my spirit above the trap of anger. Give me discernment and Your wisdom to know when I'm about to be snared by anger, and help me embrace Your peace instead.

PRAYER REQUESTS

PRAISES

ANSWERS TO PRAYER

Sunday, August 15

We know how much God loves us, and we have put our trust in his love. God is love, and all who live in love live in God, and God lives in them.

1 John 4:16 NLT

Father God, there are so many people who don't know You love them. Today I pray that Your Spirit speaks to them in a way that they might understand Your great love. Let me be a witness to that fact and help them know You as their Lord and Savior.

ANSWERS TO PRAYER

PRAYER REQUESTS

PRAISES

Monday, August 16

This is a good life—my heart is glad, my soul is full of joy, and my body is at rest. Who could want for more?
PSALM 16:9 VOICE

My body, mind, and spirit long for deep rest, Father. But I know I'm guilty of burning the candle at both ends much of the time. Help me pause every day and rest in You, knowing that You have good things—the best things—for my life.

PRAYER REQUESTS

ANSWERS TO PRAYER

PRAISES

Tuesday, August 17

For Christ himself has brought peace to us. He united Jews and Gentiles into one people when, in his own body on the cross, he broke down the wall of hostility that separated us.

Ephesians 2:14 NLT

Jesus, although I wasn't physically born into Your bloodline, You made a way for our Father God to adopt me as Your beloved sister and heir to Your kingdom. Thank You for being the uniting, peacemaking Savior of the world!

PRAYER REQUESTS

ANSWERS TO PRAYER

PRAISES

Wednesday, August 18

Whoever is generous to the poor lends to the Lord,
and he will repay him for his deed.
Proverbs 19:17 esv

God, when I acknowledge that everything I have is from You, it makes me want to be more generous with my time, possessions, and finances. Without Your gift of grace and promise of heaven, nothing I have or do today matters. When You call me to give, let me answer the call immediately and generously. I know You will multiply that blessing for me and for others!

PRAYER REQUESTS

ANSWERS TO PRAYER

PRAISES

Thursday, August 19

The LORD is good to everyone. He showers compassion on all his creation.
PSALM 145:9 NLT

I experience the truth of Your goodness every moment, Father. But there are people I know who don't believe You are good because they've had terrible things happen to them. Give me the right words and a way to share Your goodness with these people. Not in a preachy way, but in an authentic way that helps them understand that Your ultimate plan is perfectly good.

ANSWERS TO PRAYER

PRAYER REQUESTS

PRAISES

Friday, August 20

It is impossible to please God without faith. Anyone who wants to come to him must believe that God exists and that he rewards those who sincerely seek him.
HEBREWS 11:6 NLT

Lord, I lift up my family members and close friends who need to take a step toward You in faith. Some don't even have the basic belief that You exist. Show them Your glory and let them feel Your love. Only Your love can cause their hearts to seek You.

PRAYER REQUESTS

PRAISES

ANSWERS TO PRAYER

Saturday, August 21

And so, dear brothers and sisters, I plead with you to give your bodies to God because of all he has done for you. Let them be a living and holy sacrifice—the kind he will find acceptable. This is truly the way to worship him.

ROMANS 12:1 NLT

You created me for a beautiful purpose, Lord—body, heart, mind, and soul. I give these all back to You as a sacrifice of thanks for all You've done for me. Use me for Your glory!

ANSWERS TO PRAYER

PRAYER REQUESTS

PRAISES

Sunday, August 22

A true friend loves regardless of the situation,
and a real brother exists to share the tough times.
PROVERBS 17:17 VOICE

Jesus, thank You for being the example of a true friend. On earth, You loved and aided and walked alongside anyone who needed You—regardless of their backstory or failures or desperate state. And You do the same for me through every difficult season and tough time. Show me how to do the same for others!

PRAYER REQUESTS

ANSWERS TO PRAYER

PRAISES

Monday, August 23

Always be joyful. Never stop praying.
1 Thessalonians 5:16–17 NLT

I come to You every day, Jesus, praying over so many needs in my life and the lives of the people dear to me. When I'm tempted to get weighed down by the struggles I feel and see, remind me of the truth that You hold the world in Your capable hands. You care about everything from the big things to the small details, and You are faithful to take care of us all.

ANSWERS TO PRAYER

PRAYER REQUESTS

PRAISES

Tuesday, August 24

Flee youthful passions and pursue righteousness, faith, love, and peace, along with those who call on the Lord from a pure heart.

2 Timothy 2:22 ESV

Lord, I admit there have been times in my life when I was the antagonist. Especially when I was young and immature, I got a kick out of pushing the buttons of a sibling or a parent—creating chaos instead of calm. Now as I mature and grow, I will pursue the things that promote Your goodness.

PRAYER REQUESTS

ANSWERS TO PRAYER

PRAISES

Wednesday, August 25

But think about this: while we were wasting our lives in sin, God revealed His powerful love to us in a tangible display—the Anointed One died for us.
Romans 5:8 voice

It's amazing to think how You proved Your love to me before I was born, Jesus. I don't understand how, but You thought of *me* as You were on the cross. Your love, Lord, is the most powerful force in all creation, and it holds, heals, restores, and renews me every day.

ANSWERS TO PRAYER

PRAYER REQUESTS

PRAISES

Thursday, August 26

Blessed are those you choose and bring near to live in your courts!
We are filled with the good things of your house, of your holy temple.
Psalm 65:4 NIV

Father, please bless my faithfulness in doing life with my local church. It's not that you keep attendance records, but when I make it a priority to meet regularly with my church community, You are pleased! I am blessed to hear Your Word being preached, and I am encouraged to sing praises alongside other believers.

PRAYER REQUESTS

PRAISES

ANSWERS TO PRAYER

Friday, August 27

"Praise the Lord *who has given rest to his people Israel, just as he promised. Not one word has failed of all the wonderful promises he gave through his servant Moses."*

1 Kings 8:56 NLT

I am so thankful that You have already delivered on many of Your promises, Lord. But there are many things You said you'll do that are still to come. I trust that You're working these out now, and I look forward to each fulfilled promise. You have never failed Your children!

PRAYER REQUESTS

ANSWERS TO PRAYER

PRAISES

Saturday, August 28

My dear brothers and sisters, take note of this: Everyone should be quick to listen, slow to speak and slow to become angry.
James 1:19 NIV

Everyone around me is shouting to be heard, Lord. Sometimes I buy into the lie that in order to make a difference, I need to shout too. But when everyone is yelling, that means that no one is listening. Give me wisdom with my words, actions, and attitudes.

PRAYER REQUESTS

ANSWERS TO PRAYER

PRAISES

Sunday, August 29

God demonstrates his own love for us in this:
While we were still sinners, Christ died for us.
Romans 5:8 NIV

Jesus, You laid down Your life for me before I ever took a breath. Long before I realized my sinful state or asked for Your forgiveness, You'd already shown me that You love me by dying on the cross. Do I deserve that love? Absolutely not. Am I thankful for that love? Absolutely yes and amen!

ANSWERS TO PRAYER

PRAYER REQUESTS

PRAISES

Monday, August 30

I am overwhelmed with joy in the Lord *my God! For he has dressed me with the clothing of salvation and draped me in a robe of righteousness. I am like a bridegroom dressed for his wedding or a bride with her jewels.*

Isaiah 61:10 NLT

When I'm feeling down on myself, remind me that I am beautifully clothed by Your goodness, Lord! Your love and forgiveness make me worthy and welcomed into Your family, where I am Your cherished daughter.

PRAYER REQUESTS

ANSWERS TO PRAYER

PRAISES

Tuesday, August 31

Keep my commands in your heart, for they will prolong your life many years and bring you peace and prosperity.
PROVERBS 3:1–2 NIV

I am learning more each day to love Your commandments, Lord! Because even though the world says Your laws keep me in bondage, I know the truth: The key to freedom is found in obeying You. Bless my efforts to follow Your commands, and encourage me to keep going when I fail You.

ANSWERS TO PRAYER

PRAYER REQUESTS

PRAISES

SEPTEMBER 2027

"The harvest is great, but the workers are few. So pray to the Lord who is in charge of the harvest; ask him to send more workers into his fields."
LUKE 10:2 NLT

SUNDAY	MONDAY	TUESDAY	WEDNESDAY	THURSDAY	FRIDAY	SATURDAY
			1	2	3	4
5	6 Labor Day	7	8	9	10	11
12	13	14	15	16	17	18
19	20	21	22	23 First Day of Autumn	24	25
26	27	28	29	30		

Our prayers should always include what Jesus specifically said to pray for. Let's not forget what He taught when sending out His first disciples: How great the harvest but how few are those willing to help lead people to salvation in Him. May we constantly remember to pray for more willing and eager workers—and to be them ourselves.

Wednesday, September 1

Let us give thanks all the time to God through Jesus Christ. Our gift to Him is to give thanks. Our lips should always give thanks to His name. Remember to do good and help each other. Gifts like this please God.

HEBREWS 13:15–16 NLV

You are so kind and loving, Lord, and You want me to worship and give back to You by sharing Your kindness with others. It's an honor to know, love, and follow You!

ANSWERS TO PRAYER

PRAYER REQUESTS

PRAISES

Thursday, September 2

A single day in your courts is better than a thousand anywhere else! I would rather be a gatekeeper in the house of my God than live the good life in the homes of the wicked.

PSALM 84:10 NLT

The goodness that comes from You is infinitely better than any of the world's sinful ideas of good, Lord. Keep me safe and secure in this truth all my days! I never want to leave You to follow the world.

PRAYER REQUESTS

ANSWERS TO PRAYER

PRAISES

Friday, September 3

Let those who love the Lord hate evil, for he guards the lives of his faithful ones and delivers them from the hand of the wicked. Light shines on the righteous and joy on the upright in heart.

Psalm 97:10–11 NIV

Lord, let all of us who love and follow You hate evil and faithfully stand against it. You will guard and protect us; we have nothing to fear. Let Your light shine through us to pierce the darkness, and let us help lead others out of it, toward Your love and grace.

PRAYER REQUESTS

ANSWERS TO PRAYER

PRAISES

Saturday, September 4

Do not bring sorrow to God's Holy Spirit by the way you live. Remember, he has identified you as his own, guaranteeing that you will be saved on the day of redemption. Get rid of all bitterness, rage, anger, harsh words, and slander, as well as all types of evil behavior. Instead, be kind to each other, tenderhearted, forgiving one another, just as God through Christ has forgiven you.

EPHESIANS 4:30–32 NLT

Lord, I want self-control so that I don't bring sorrow to You. No one loves and cares for me like You do, and I want to please You and praise You with my life!

PRAYER REQUESTS

ANSWERS TO PRAYER

PRAISES

Sunday, September 5

And this is my prayer: that your love may abound more and more in knowledge and depth of insight, so that you may be able to discern what is best and may be pure and blameless for the day of Christ, filled with the fruit of righteousness that comes through Jesus Christ—to the glory and praise of God.

PHILIPPIANS 1:9–11 NIV

Lord, increase my love for You and others. Let it "abound more and more in knowledge and depth of insight." Your true, genuine love is the only kind I want.

ANSWERS TO PRAYER

PRAYER REQUESTS

PRAISES

Monday, September 6

LABOR DAY

Therefore, since we have been made right in God's sight by faith, we have peace with God because of what Jesus Christ our Lord has done for us. Because of our faith, Christ has brought us into this place of undeserved privilege where we now stand, and we confidently and joyfully look forward to sharing God's glory.

ROMANS 5:1–2 NLT

Dear Jesus, I'm so blessed and full of joy right now because of the peace and privilege I have since You saved me from sin. I am so excited that there's even greater joy ahead for eternity with You!

PRAYER REQUESTS

ANSWERS TO PRAYER

PRAISES

Tuesday, September 7

Work for the things that make peace and help each other become stronger Christians.
ROMANS 14:19 NLV

Lord, I want it to be true of me and of all my brothers and sisters in Christ—among my family, friends, church family, and community—that we strive to make peace and to help one another become stronger in our love and service to You. Help me do all I can to encourage this!

ANSWERS TO PRAYER

PRAYER REQUESTS

PRAISES

Wednesday, September 8

Thomas said to Jesus, "Lord, we do not know where You are going. How can we know the way to get there?" Jesus said, "I am the Way and the Truth and the Life. No one can go to the Father except by Me."
JOHN 14:5–6 NLV

Jesus, remind me regularly that there is nothing kinder I can do for others than to point them to You as the way, the truth, and the life!

PRAYER REQUESTS

PRAISES

ANSWERS TO PRAYER

Thursday, September 9

God saved you by his grace when you believed. And you can't take credit for this; it is a gift from God. Salvation is not a reward for the good things we have done, so none of us can boast about it. For we are God's masterpiece. He has created us anew in Christ Jesus, so we can do the good things he planned for us long ago.

EPHESIANS 2:8–10 NLT

Every good thing I do is because You have saved me from sin and planned good things for me. Thank You, Lord!

ANSWERS TO PRAYER

PRAYER REQUESTS

PRAISES

Friday, September 10

Love the LORD, all his faithful people! The LORD preserves those who are true to him, but the proud he pays back in full. Be strong and take heart, all you who hope in the LORD.

PSALM 31:23–24 NIV

Keep me strong in heart as I fall more and more in love with You, Lord. Above all else, I want to be faithful and true to You!

PRAYER REQUESTS

ANSWERS TO PRAYER

PRAISES

Saturday, September 11

Don't you realize that in a race everyone runs, but only one person gets the prize? So run to win! All athletes are disciplined in their training. They do it to win a prize that will fade away, but we do it for an eternal prize.

1 Corinthians 9:24–25 NLT

Dear God, help me to have good self-control and discipline like an excellent athlete, knowing the blessings and promises from You are far better than any worldly achievement.

ANSWERS TO PRAYER

PRAYER REQUESTS

PRAISES

Sunday, September 12

Flee the evil desires of youth and pursue righteousness, faith, love and peace, along with those who call on the Lord out of a pure heart.
2 Timothy 2:22 NIV

Lord, I don't want the worldly, sinful ideas of love that are so often rooted in evil, selfishness, and lust. Help me flee all that and pursue *genuine* righteousness, faith, love, and peace—genuine because they match what You say about these virtues.

PRAYER REQUESTS

PRAISES

ANSWERS TO PRAYER

Monday, September 13

Do everything without complaining and arguing, so that no one can criticize you. Live clean, innocent lives as children of God, shining like bright lights in a world full of crooked and perverse people.

PHILIPPIANS 2:14–15 NLT

God, help me to do even the small and unpleasant tasks of life without grumbling. Let me be a shining light that shares the joy, hope, and peace that come from You in any situation.

PRAYER REQUESTS

ANSWERS TO PRAYER

PRAISES

Tuesday, September 14

Unfailing love and faithfulness make atonement for sin.
By fearing the LORD, people avoid evil. When people's lives please
the LORD, even their enemies are at peace with them.
PROVERBS 16:6–7 NLT

Dear Lord, I want my life to please You. Show me how I need to change and obey You better. Please forgive me for my sin and bring peace in all areas of my life.

PRAYER REQUESTS

PRAISES

ANSWERS TO PRAYER

Wednesday, September 15

I waited patiently for the LORD; he inclined to me and heard my cry. He drew me up from the pit of destruction, out of the miry bog, and set my feet upon a rock, making my steps secure. He put a new song in my mouth, a song of praise to our God. Many will see and fear, and put their trust in the LORD.

PSALM 40:1–3 ESV

Lord, when I'm patient and receive blessings in Your perfect timing, please help others to notice. Let that inspire more patience and trust in You.

ANSWERS TO PRAYER

PRAYER REQUESTS

PRAISES

Thursday, September 16

You have done many good things for me, LORD, just as you promised.
I believe in your commands; now teach me good judgment and knowledge.
I used to wander off until you disciplined me; but now I closely follow
your word. You are good and do only good; teach me your decrees.
PSALM 119:65–68 NLT

Good and only good—that's such a great way to describe You, Lord. You do only good things, and You help me do them as well. I'm so grateful I get to follow You!

PRAYER REQUESTS

ANSWERS TO PRAYER

PRAISES

Friday, September 17

You have every spiritual gift you need as you eagerly wait for the return of our Lord Jesus Christ. He will keep you strong to the end so that you will be free from all blame on the day when our Lord Jesus Christ returns. God will do this, for he is faithful to do what he says, and he has invited you into partnership with his Son, Jesus Christ our Lord.

1 CORINTHIANS 1:7–9 NLT

You are so faithful to do what You say, Lord. I believe You and Your Word, and I praise You for being my hope, my strength, my salvation!

ANSWERS TO PRAYER

PRAYER REQUESTS

PRAISES

Saturday, September 18

Those who consider themselves religious and yet do not keep a tight rein on their tongues deceive themselves, and their religion is worthless. Religion that God our Father accepts as pure and faultless is this: to look after orphans and widows in their distress and to keep oneself from being polluted by the world.

James 1:26–27 NIV

Lord, help me have good control over what I say. Help me live out my faith by avoiding sin and taking care of those in need.

PRAYER REQUESTS

ANSWERS TO PRAYER

PRAISES

Sunday, September 19

If you have any encouragement from being united with Christ, if any comfort from his love, if any common sharing in the Spirit, if any tenderness and compassion, then make my joy complete by being like-minded, having the same love, being one in spirit and of one mind.

PHILIPPIANS 2:1–2 NIV

Dear Jesus, I have endless love and encouragement from being united with You! Help me spread that love and encouragement to everyone around me.

ANSWERS TO PRAYER

PRAYER REQUESTS

PRAISES

Monday, September 20

All Scripture is inspired by God and is useful to teach us what is true and to make us realize what is wrong in our lives. It corrects us when we are wrong and teaches us to do what is right. God uses it to prepare and equip his people to do every good work.
2 Timothy 3:16–17 NLT

Your Word gives me joy, Lord! Thank You for teaching, guiding, preparing, and equipping me through it.

PRAYER REQUESTS

ANSWERS TO PRAYER

PRAISES

Tuesday, September 21

Those who plant seeds of peace will gather what is right and good.
James 3:18 NLV

Lord, I don't always feel like doing the peaceful, calm thing. I'm often tempted to give in to angry words and actions when I'm upset. Please forgive me. Help me remember that when I choose Your ways and decide to plant seeds of peace instead of anger, strife, and sin, I won't regret it. I'll end up blessed instead of stressed.

ANSWERS TO PRAYER

PRAYER REQUESTS

PRAISES

Wednesday, September 22

He will swallow up death forever; and the LORD GOD will wipe away tears from all faces, and the reproach of his people he will take away from all the earth, for the LORD has spoken. It will be said on that day, "Behold, this is our God; we have waited for him, that he might save us. This is the LORD; we have waited for him; let us be glad and rejoice in his salvation."

ISAIAH 25:8–9 ESV

Lord God, I will trust and wait on You because I believe every word You say.

PRAYER REQUESTS

ANSWERS TO PRAYER

PRAISES

Thursday, September 23

FIRST DAY OF AUTUMN

How great is the goodness you have stored up for those who fear you. You lavish it on those who come to you for protection, blessing them before the watching world. You hide them in the shelter of your presence, safe from those who conspire against them. You shelter them in your presence, far from accusing tongues.

PSALM 31:19–20 NLT

Thank You for this promise, Lord. As You lavish Your goodness on me, help me to share it with others!

ANSWERS TO PRAYER

PRAYER REQUESTS

PRAISES

Friday, September 24

Let love and faithfulness never leave you; bind them around your neck, write them on the tablet of your heart. Then you will win favor and a good name in the sight of God and man.

Proverbs 3:3–4 niv

Lord, I want to be loving and faithful to You at all times—and I want that to impact all I do and how I interact with others. Let me lead more people to salvation in You!

PRAYER REQUESTS

ANSWERS TO PRAYER

PRAISES

Saturday, September 25

Make every effort to add to your faith goodness; and to goodness, knowledge; and to knowledge, self-control; and to self-control, perseverance; and to perseverance, godliness; and to godliness, mutual affection; and to mutual affection, love. For if you possess these qualities in increasing measure, they will keep you from being ineffective and unproductive in your knowledge of our Lord Jesus Christ.

2 Peter 1:5–8 NIV

Jesus, help me to keep growing my faith with all these good virtues. I want to be effective and productive as Your follower!

PRAYER REQUESTS

ANSWERS TO PRAYER

PRAISES

Sunday, September 26

May the Lord make your love for one another and for all people grow and overflow, just as our love for you overflows. May he, as a result, make your hearts strong, blameless, and holy as you stand before God our Father when our Lord Jesus comes again with all his holy people.
1 THESSALONIANS 3:12–13 NLT

Lord, I'm stronger and better when Your love fills me up to overflowing. Keep pouring! Thank You!

PRAYER REQUESTS

ANSWERS TO PRAYER

PRAISES

Monday, September 27

And the word of the Lord was spreading throughout the whole region. But the Jews incited the devout women of high standing and the leading men of the city, stirred up persecution against Paul and Barnabas, and drove them out of their district. But they shook off the dust from their feet against them and went to Iconium. And the disciples were filled with joy and with the Holy Spirit.

Acts 13:49–52 ESV

Lord, help me remember that even though there will always be people who will be hostile to me because I follow You, I have purpose and joy and the presence of Your Holy Spirit!

ANSWERS TO PRAYER

PRAYER REQUESTS

PRAISES

Tuesday, September 28

Watch out for people who cause divisions and upset people's faith by teaching things contrary to what you have been taught. Stay away from them. Such people are not serving Christ our Lord; they are serving their own personal interests. By smooth talk and glowing words they deceive innocent people.... I want you to be wise in doing right and to stay innocent of any wrong. The God of peace will soon crush Satan under your feet. May the grace of our Lord Jesus be with you.

ROMANS 16:17–20 NLT

God of peace, please protect me from false teaching. Keep me away from those who deceive, divide, and destroy.

PRAYER REQUESTS

PRAISES

ANSWERS TO PRAYER

Wednesday, September 29

The troubles of my heart are enlarged; bring me out of my distresses. Consider my affliction and my trouble, and forgive all my sins. Consider how many are my foes, and with what violent hatred they hate me. Oh, guard my soul, and deliver me! Let me not be put to shame, for I take refuge in you. May integrity and uprightness preserve me, for I wait for you.

Psalm 25:17–21 ESV

Dear Lord, I know You see the troubles I have, and I'm asking You to help. I trust You even if I need to be patient for a while longer. I want to wait on You well.

PRAYER REQUESTS

ANSWERS TO PRAYER

PRAISES

Thursday, September 30

Teach me to do your will, for you are my God!
Let your good Spirit lead me on level ground!
PSALM 143:10 ESV

Help me to always want Your will, Lord. Show me where my desires are faulty, and make my will match Yours. Lead me on level ground, and guide me in all the good things You have planned for me to do!

PRAYER REQUESTS

PRAISES

ANSWERS TO PRAYER

OCTOBER 2027

"The grass withers and the flowers fade,
but the word of our God stands forever."
ISAIAH 40:8 NLT

SUNDAY	MONDAY	TUESDAY	WEDNESDAY	THURSDAY	FRIDAY	SATURDAY
					1	2
3	4	5	6	7	8	9
10	11 Columbus Day	12	13	14	15	16
17	18	19	20	21	22	23
24 / Halloween 31	25	26	27	28	29	30

The world makes an unsteady foundation to build our lives on. Popular opinion, right and wrong, politics—everything changes from day to day, and if we're honest, it's all pretty confusing. The good news is that God—and His Word—are unchanging and eternal. Choose today to build your life on Him!

Friday, October 1

Our marriage will be honest and truthful, and you'll understand who I really am—the Eternal One.
HOSEA 2:20 VOICE

God, the covenant relationship You offered Israel through the prophet Hosea was a fresh start. And that's what You offer me every day—a fresh start, a clean slate. You offer me a faithful promise that You love me unconditionally and nothing can separate Your love from me. Help me to know You more and more!

PRAYER REQUESTS

PRAISES

ANSWERS TO PRAYER

Saturday, October 2

So prepare your minds for action and exercise self-control.
Put all your hope in the gracious salvation that will come
to you when Jesus Christ is revealed to the world.

1 Peter 1:13 NLT

You created me with free will, Father, but You also gave me the potential for great strength of character. I'm not perfect, and I never will be this side of heaven. But every day with Your help, I can become more sound in my thinking and have better self-control. I am not a victim of my circumstances!

ANSWERS TO PRAYER

PRAYER REQUESTS

PRAISES

Sunday, October 3

As we live in God, our love grows more perfect. So we will not be afraid on the day of judgment, but we can face him with confidence because we live like Jesus here in this world.

1 John 4:17 NLT

Lord, I'm so thankful to live in Your grace, Your love, Your peace, and Your beauty every day. That doesn't mean my life is perfect or that I'm perfect, but I have confidence that with Your direction I am becoming more like Your Son every day.

PRAYER REQUESTS

ANSWERS TO PRAYER

PRAISES

Monday, October 4

The Lord is my strength and my safe cover. My heart trusts in Him, and I am helped. So my heart is full of joy. I will thank Him with my song.
Psalm 28:7 NLV

Father, I am learning to trust You more each day. I look back at difficult seasons in my past and see how well You took care of me. You kept me safe. You shielded me from harm. And I am so thankful to know that You will do that again!

ANSWERS TO PRAYER

PRAYER REQUESTS

PRAISES

Tuesday, October 5

See that no one repays anyone evil for evil, but always seek to do good to one another and to everyone.
1 Thessalonians 5:15 ESV

When the world around me seems bent on revenge, God, help me remember that Your law is love. Revenge is simply a twisted form of justice, and it will never bring about peace or satisfaction. Instead, help me promote good and let me be strong enough to spread kindness and understanding—*especially* when I have been wronged.

PRAYER REQUESTS

ANSWERS TO PRAYER

PRAISES

Wednesday, October 6

We who have strong faith should help those who are weak. We should not live to please ourselves.
Romans 15:1 NLV

My faith in You is growing every day, Lord. I don't want to keep it just to myself, though. Please give me opportunities to encourage and mentor younger Christians as they grow in You. My experiences and my relationship with You can be a blessing to others and glorify You at the same time.

ANSWERS TO PRAYER

PRAYER REQUESTS

PRAISES

Thursday, October 7

Once you were full of darkness, but now you have light from the Lord. So live as people of light! For this light within you produces only what is good and right and true.
EPHESIANS 5:8–9 NLT

Before I knew You, Jesus, my life felt like I was groping in the dark—not really knowing my purpose. But Your light gave me direction to follow You. And since I accepted Your gift of grace, Your Spirit now shines from *me* too! May that light always lead others straight to You.

PRAYER REQUESTS

ANSWERS TO PRAYER

PRAISES

Friday, October 8

A faithful person will be richly blessed,
but one eager to get rich will not go unpunished.
PROVERBS 28:20 NIV

I've heard many get-rich-quick schemes over the years, Lord, but the truth is that if something sounds too good to be true, it probably isn't a wise idea. Give me the wisdom and desire to work hard in all I do, because I know You are faithful to bless my efforts.

PRAYER REQUESTS

ANSWERS TO PRAYER

PRAISES

Saturday, October 9

Set a guard over my mouth, Lord; keep watch over the door of my lips.
Psalm 141:3 NIV

Just like David, the writer of Psalm 141, I know my words are impossible to tame by myself. I've tried too many times to be the be the doorkeeper of my lips—and failed! So, God, please be the Lord of my words. Prick my conscience before I let hurt fly out of my mouth. Help me choose words that will help and heal.

PRAYER REQUESTS

ANSWERS TO PRAYER

PRAISES

Sunday, October 10

There is no greater way to love than to give your life for your friends.
John 15:13 voice

Jesus, You show me the greatest love through Your every word and action—especially Your work on the cross. Although I may never have to physically die to help a friend, I will die to my selfishness, die to always being right, and die to my ego in order to love others more like You do.

ANSWERS TO PRAYER

PRAYER REQUESTS

PRAISES

Monday, October 11

COLUMBUS DAY

Clap your hands, all peoples! Shout to God with loud songs of joy!
PSALM 47:1 ESV

When I think about what You've done for me, Lord, praise bubbles up from within me. When I see a gorgeous sunrise, I can't help but raise my hands in worship of Your magnificence. When I feel Your Spirit move in my heart, a melody rises from my lungs. You are my good, good Father!

PRAYER REQUESTS

ANSWERS TO PRAYER

PRAISES

Tuesday, October 12

Eternal One, You are preparing peace for us; in fact, everything we have accomplished has come from You.
Isaiah 26:12 voice

When I experience even a moment of Your peace, Lord, I realize how much I truly need more of it in my life! The whole world needs Your peace. Teach me, Father, the pathway to Your unending supply of peace. Let me experience it more and more as my faith grows and I learn to be more like Jesus.

ANSWERS TO PRAYER

PRAYER REQUESTS

PRAISES

Wednesday, October 13

May God, who gives this patience and encouragement, help you live in complete harmony with each other, as is fitting for followers of Christ Jesus.
ROMANS 15:5 NLT

Lord, please bless my church with a unified spirit. We are imperfect people with many different personalities and opinions, and only Your love can unite us and make our differences sing harmoniously together. Teach us how to serve one another so the world will see what You are all about, Jesus.

PRAYER REQUESTS

PRAISES

ANSWERS TO PRAYER

Thursday, October 14

God can give you all you need. He will give you more than enough. You will have everything you need for yourselves. And you will have enough left over to give when there is a need.

2 Corinthians 9:8 NLV

You are such a generous God! Even when the budget is extra tight, You are always faithful to supply everything I need. Open my eyes to the needs of others around me. Show me how I can be Your hands and feet and meet those needs.

ANSWERS TO PRAYER

PRAYER REQUESTS

PRAISES

Friday, October 15

You have never been tempted to sin in any different way than other people. God is faithful. He will not allow you to be tempted more than you can take. But when you are tempted, He will make a way for you to keep from falling into sin.

1 Corinthians 10:13 NLV

When I am tempted to sin, Father, help me see the path You are providing for me to resist. You cheer for me to make the right choice, and You'll faithfully bless me when I do!

PRAYER REQUESTS

ANSWERS TO PRAYER

PRAISES

Saturday, October 16

A fool is quick-tempered, but a wise person stays calm when insulted.
PROVERBS 12:16 NLT

When someone insults me, I feel hurt to the bottom of my soul, Lord. How can I rise above that and remain calm? Although You endured mockery, You knew the truth of who You were and that Your Father God was on Your side. Even when insults and ridicule were hurled at You as You headed toward the cross, You did not retaliate.

ANSWERS TO PRAYER

PRAYER REQUESTS

PRAISES

Sunday, October 17

Hatred stirs up conflict, but love covers over all wrongs.
PROVERBS 10:12 NIV

Lord, I admit that my knee-jerk reaction to someone who upsets me is not always love. Honestly, my reaction is *rarely* love. When someone does something that angers me, remind me to pause. Help me breathe in Your Spirit of peace so I can recall the wisdom of Proverbs 10:12. A love-prompted response in Your name, Father, can soothe and unite, heal and promote peace.

PRAYER REQUESTS

ANSWERS TO PRAYER

PRAISES

Monday, October 18

I receive joy when I am weak. I receive joy when people talk against me and make it hard for me and try to hurt me and make trouble for me. I receive joy when all these things come to me because of Christ. For when I am weak, then I am strong.

2 Corinthians 12:10 NLV

Lord, teach me to be joyful in the middle of difficulties. Show me Your power when I'm weak. Please stay near me no matter what.

ANSWERS TO PRAYER

PRAYER REQUESTS

PRAISES

Tuesday, October 19

Look at those who are honest and good, for a wonderful future awaits those who love peace.
Psalm 37:37 NLT

Lord, thank You for the good, godly people You've put in my life—the ones whose examples I can follow, because I know they are following hard after You! These mentors are an encouragement to me, and even though they're not perfect, I see how they navigate difficult times with strength and reliance on Your Spirit.

PRAYER REQUESTS

PRAISES

ANSWERS TO PRAYER

Wednesday, October 20

A soft answer turns away wrath, but a harsh word stirs up anger.
PROVERBS 15:1 ESV

You give me many opportunities to respond to others every day, Lord. I'll answer a request from a family member or interact with a coworker, someone online, or the person behind me at the check-out. In each of these situations, I can choose to be kind and patient or rude and indifferent. Help me choose Your way.

ANSWERS TO PRAYER

PRAYER REQUESTS

PRAISES

Thursday, October 21

Turn away from evil and do good; seek peace and pursue it.
Psalm 34:14 ESV

Father God, please bless my friendships. Align me with others who passionately pursue You so that we are headed in the same direction. And with my friends who have yet to find You, let me shine Your light in their dark moments—let me be the person who shows them the way to You. Show me the good You have for me, Lord, and I will do it!

PRAYER REQUESTS

PRAISES

ANSWERS TO PRAYER

Friday, October 22

The faithful love of the LORD never ends! His mercies never cease. Great is his faithfulness; his mercies begin afresh each morning.
LAMENTATIONS 3:22–23 NLT

You breathe new life into our relationship every day, Father. As morning dawns, so does the chance for me to lean into Your grace, Your mercy, Your life-giving love for me. You sustain me through each day, Lord, and I am learning—little by little—to trust You more!

ANSWERS TO PRAYER

PRAYER REQUESTS

PRAISES

Saturday, October 23

Do not veer off course to the right or the left;
step away from evil, and leave it behind.
Proverbs 4:27 VOICE

I've believed the lies for too long, Father. Today I choose to turn my back on that sin—that temptation that trips me up too easily—and leave it behind. I'm back on Your lighted path, Lord, and I will put one foot in front of the other, running straight from evil and into Your arms.

PRAYER REQUESTS

PRAISES

ANSWERS TO PRAYER

Sunday, October 24

There is no fear in love. Perfect love puts fear out of our hearts.
1 John 4:18 NLV

I see so much fear in the world around me every day, Jesus. And I admit that the world's darkness often tries to permeate my soul with that fear. Reassure my mind and heart that because You love me with perfect love, I have no reason to be afraid! I want to show the people around me the perfect peace that comes with living for You, Lord.

ANSWERS TO PRAYER

PRAYER REQUESTS

PRAISES

Monday, October 25

Your words became a joy to me and the happiness of my heart.
For I have been called by Your name, O Lord God of All.
Jeremiah 15:16 NLV

The more I read the Bible, Lord, the more I fall in love with Your Word! Thank You for loving Your children so much that You gave us a way to hear from You, know You more, and learn the life-giving wisdom of scripture. Your Word illuminates my life.

PRAYER REQUESTS

ANSWERS TO PRAYER

PRAISES

Tuesday, October 26

Try to understand other people. Forgive each other. If you have something against someone, forgive him. That is the way the Lord forgave you.
Colossians 3:13 NLV

Jesus, there are a few people around me I simply cannot understand. I don't know why they do what they do or what they're thinking. Truthfully, I'd like to cut them out of my life, but that's not what You want. You call me to work toward understanding, forgiveness, and peace. With Your help, I will try, Lord!

PRAYER REQUESTS

ANSWERS TO PRAYER

PRAISES

Wednesday, October 27

Of what great worth is Your loving-kindness, O God!
The children of men come and are safe in the shadow of Your wings.
PSALM 36:7 NLV

Father, thank You for keeping me safe. And it's not just from physical harm. When I live according to Your Word, I am less likely to be in situations that tempt me to sin. When I'm in tune with Your Spirit, I make wiser choices, love others better, and reap the benefits of right living.

PRAYER REQUESTS

ANSWERS TO PRAYER

PRAISES

Thursday, October 28

You know God identified Jesus as the uniquely chosen One by pouring out the Holy Spirit on Him, by empowering Him. You know Jesus went through the land doing good for all and healing all who were suffering under the oppression of the evil one, for God was with Him.

Acts 10:38 voice

Father, thank You for the gift of the Holy Spirit. It's incredible to realize that the same Spirit who empowered Jesus while He was on earth now lives in *me*!

ANSWERS TO PRAYER

PRAYER REQUESTS

PRAISES

Friday, October 29

Your steadfast love, O Lord, extends to the heavens, your faithfulness to the clouds.
Psalm 36:5 ESV

So many relationships seem to be expendable, Lord. Every day, promises go unfulfilled, feelings change, vows are broken, and people move on. Yet Your relationship with me is unchanging. It is cemented. It is forever. Thank You for Your faithful commitment to me, to my salvation, and to making me a home with You for eternity.

PRAYER REQUESTS

ANSWERS TO PRAYER

PRAISES

Saturday, October 30

Dear brothers and sisters, if another believer is overcome by some sin, you who are godly should gently and humbly help that person back onto the right path. And be careful not to fall into the same temptation yourself.

Galatians 6:1 NLT

My friend is making poor decisions, Lord, and I so desperately want to help her. I know she loves You, but she seems blind and deaf to Your teaching right now. Show me how to help her, how to love her back onto Your righteous path.

ANSWERS TO PRAYER

PRAYER REQUESTS

PRAISES

Sunday, October 31

HALLOWEEN

No power in the sky above or in the earth below—indeed, nothing in all creation will ever be able to separate us from the love of God that is revealed in Christ Jesus our Lord.

Romans 8:39 NLT

Your love is the most powerful force in the world, Father, overcoming and enduring through everything You created—both in the physical and spiritual realms. I have nothing to fear because I am surrounded by Your love on every side, every day and in every way.

PRAYER REQUESTS

ANSWERS TO PRAYER

PRAISES

NOVEMBER 2027

Do not worry. Learn to pray about everything. Give thanks to God as you ask Him for what you need. The peace of God. . . will keep your hearts and minds through Christ Jesus.

PHILIPPIANS 4:6–7 NLV

SUNDAY	MONDAY	TUESDAY	WEDNESDAY	THURSDAY	FRIDAY	SATURDAY
	1	2 Election Day	3	4	5	6
7 Daylight Saving Time Ends	8	9	10	11 Veterans Day	12	13
14	15	16	17	18	19	20
21	22	23	24	25 Thanksgiving	26	27
28	29	30				

There is no stress-free life. But we can have a worry-free life when we daily pray about everything, telling God what we need and never forgetting to *give thanks* for all He's done and will do. "No worries" is a trendy thing to say, but as Christians we can truly live it!

Monday, November 1

Though you have not seen him, you love him; and even though you do not see him now, you believe in him and are filled with an inexpressible and glorious joy, for you are receiving the end result of your faith, the salvation of your souls.

1 PETER 1:8–9 NIV

Lord, I love You. Even though I can't see You in the physical sense, I see You in all the ways that matter most. I know You are present, and You're working in my life and in the world around me. Thank You for saving me and filling me with joy!

PRAYER REQUESTS

ANSWERS TO PRAYER

PRAISES

Tuesday, November 2

ELECTION DAY

Don't worry about anything; instead, pray about everything. Tell God what you need, and thank him for all he has done. Then you will experience God's peace, which exceeds anything we can understand. His peace will guard your hearts and minds as you live in Christ Jesus.

PHILIPPIANS 4:6–7 NLT

Lord, Your perfect peace is truly amazing and otherworldly. Thank You for letting me experience it when I choose to pray to You about all my needs and hopes. Thank You for all You've already done and provided.

ANSWERS TO PRAYER

PRAYER REQUESTS

PRAISES

Wednesday, November 3

Finally, all of you, have unity of mind, sympathy, brotherly love, a tender heart, and a humble mind. Do not repay evil for evil or reviling for reviling, but on the contrary, bless, for to this you were called, that you may obtain a blessing.

1 Peter 3:8–9 ESV

Remind me what I'm called to, Lord—to love like You do, with patience, kindness, tenderness, humility, and blessing. Keep me learning and growing in Your real love.

PRAYER REQUESTS

ANSWERS TO PRAYER

PRAISES

Thursday, November 4

The faithful love of the LORD never ends! His mercies never cease. Great is his faithfulness; his mercies begin afresh each morning. I say to myself, "The LORD is my inheritance; therefore, I will hope in him!" The LORD is good to those who depend on him, to those who search for him. So it is good to wait quietly for salvation from the LORD.

LAMENTATIONS 3:22–26 NLT

Your goodness is limitless, Lord! I'm so grateful for the mercy and salvation You offer to anyone who trusts in You.

ANSWERS TO PRAYER

PRAYER REQUESTS

PRAISES

Friday, November 5

Send me your light and your faithful care, let them lead me; let them bring me to your holy mountain, to the place where you dwell. Then I will go to the altar of God, to God, my joy and my delight. I will praise you with the lyre, O God, my God.

PSALM 43:3–4 NIV

Sometimes I feel like I'm in dreary darkness, Lord. When I'm in that place, please send your light and Your faithful care to lead me back to You. I need the perfect peace, comfort, and joy that are only possible when I'm close to You!

PRAYER REQUESTS

PRAISES

ANSWERS TO PRAYER

Saturday, November 6

At the same time, pray also for us, that God may open to us a door for the word, to declare the mystery of Christ, on account of which I am in prison—that I may make it clear, which is how I ought to speak. Walk in wisdom toward outsiders, making the best use of the time. Let your speech always be gracious, seasoned with salt, so that you may know how you ought to answer each person.

Colossians 4:3–6 ESV

Lord, give me extra self-control and wisdom to help draw unbelievers to You.

ANSWERS TO PRAYER

PRAYER REQUESTS

PRAISES

Sunday, November 7

DAYLIGHT SAVING TIME ENDS

The Lord is faithful, and he will strengthen you and protect you from the evil one. We have confidence in the Lord that you are doing and will continue to do the things we command. May the Lord direct your hearts into God's love and Christ's perseverance.

2 Thessalonians 3:3–5 NIV

I want my heart directed into Your love every moment, Lord. It's because of You that I am protected from evil and can persevere in this sinful world. It's because of You that I can share Your love, truth, and salvation with others.

PRAYER REQUESTS

ANSWERS TO PRAYER

PRAISES

Monday, November 8

Jesus Christ is the same yesterday and today and forever.
HEBREWS 13:8 ESV

Dear Jesus, it's easy to get caught up in uncertainty and anxiety and let them steal my joy. When I'm tempted to worry and despair, I need to remember the truth that You never change. You are the same good God in the past, present, and future. You know me, love me, and take good care of me—both now and forever. What peace and joy that gives me. Thank You and hallelujah!

PRAYER REQUESTS

ANSWERS TO PRAYER

PRAISES

Tuesday, November 9

Jesus looked at them and said, "With man this is impossible, but with God all things are possible."
Matthew 19:26 NIV

When I'm tempted to worry and fret about how a situation will possibly be resolved or how a need will ever be provided for, remind me of Your words in this Scripture. Absolutely anything is possible for You, God. I have no reason to fear and every reason for peace because I trust in You!

PRAYER REQUESTS

ANSWERS TO PRAYER

PRAISES

Wednesday, November 10

Be still before the Lord *and wait patiently for him; fret not yourself over the one who prospers in his way, over the man who carries out evil devices! Refrain from anger, and forsake wrath! Fret not yourself; it tends only to evil. For the evildoers shall be cut off, but those who wait for the* Lord *all inherit the land.*

Psalm 37:7–9 esv

Lord, help me focus on You while I wait for Your answers and blessing. Help me ignore those around me who seem to prosper even though they reject You. I trust Your timing and Your perfect, true prosperity.

ANSWERS TO PRAYER

PRAYER REQUESTS

PRAISES

Thursday, November 11

VETERANS DAY

The LORD is my shepherd; I have all that I need. He lets me rest in green meadows; he leads me beside peaceful streams. He renews my strength. He guides me along right paths, bringing honor to his name. . . . Surely your goodness and unfailing love will pursue me all the days of my life, and I will live in the house of the LORD forever.

PSALM 23:1–3, 6 NLT

Jesus, my shepherd, thank You! Because of You, I have every bit of goodness I'll ever need—now and forever.

PRAYER REQUESTS

ANSWERS TO PRAYER

PRAISES

Friday, November 12

This is a trustworthy saying: If we die with him, we will also live with him. If we endure hardship, we will reign with him. If we deny him, he will deny us. If we are unfaithful, he remains faithful, for he cannot deny who he is.

2 Timothy 2:11–13 NLT

You are endlessly, unfailingly faithful, Lord. There is no one like You, and I worship and live for You alone!

ANSWERS TO PRAYER

PRAYER REQUESTS

PRAISES

Saturday, November 13

He said to Jesus, "I will give You all these nations if You will get down at my feet and worship me." Jesus said to the devil, "Get away, Satan. It is written, 'You must worship the Lord your God. You must obey Him only.'" Then the devil went away from Jesus. Angels came and cared for Him.

MATTHEW 4:9–11 NLV

Jesus, I know Satan will try to tempt me too. Help me remember Your example, be equipped with Your Word, and have self-control to resist him and tell him to flee!

PRAYER REQUESTS

ANSWERS TO PRAYER

PRAISES

Sunday, November 14

We will speak the truth in love, growing in every way more and more like Christ, who is the head of his body, the church. He makes the whole body fit together perfectly. As each part does its own special work, it helps the other parts grow, so that the whole body is healthy and growing and full of love.
Ephesians 4:15–16 NLT

Lord, keep me in tune with You, speaking Your truth in love *when* and *where* and *how* You want me to.

ANSWERS TO PRAYER

PRAYER REQUESTS

PRAISES

Monday, November 15

Always be joyful. Never stop praying. Be thankful in all circumstances, for this is God's will for you who belong to Christ Jesus.
1 Thessalonians 5:16–18 NLT

Lord, sometimes it sounds impossible to always be joyful. But then I realize that if I never stop praying and never stop being thankful, I can't help but be joyful—because I'll be constantly talking to and praising You. All real joy is in Your presence, and I'm so grateful I can come to You!

PRAYER REQUESTS

ANSWERS TO PRAYER

PRAISES

Tuesday, November 16

He says, "Be still, and know that I am God; I will be exalted among the nations, I will be exalted in the earth." The Lord *Almighty is with us; the God of Jacob is our fortress.*

Psalm 46:10–11 niv

Almighty God, help me remember to be still and silent and focus on Your greatness! You are always right here with me through Your Holy Spirit.

PRAYER REQUESTS

ANSWERS TO PRAYER

PRAISES

Wednesday, November 17

"Do not be anxious, saying, 'What shall we eat?' or 'What shall we drink?' or 'What shall we wear?' For the Gentiles seek after all these things, and your heavenly Father knows that you need them all. But seek first the kingdom of God and his righteousness, and all these things will be added to you."
MATTHEW 6:31–33 ESV

Dear Jesus, I'm sorry I worry about things too often. Thank You for Your patience with me. Help me simply to seek Your kingdom first, because You know my every need and You have everything under control.

PRAYER REQUESTS

PRAISES

ANSWERS TO PRAYER

Thursday, November 18

Let each generation tell its children of your mighty acts; let them proclaim your power. I will meditate on your majestic, glorious splendor and your wonderful miracles. Your awe-inspiring deeds will be on every tongue; I will proclaim your greatness. Everyone will share the story of your wonderful goodness; they will sing with joy about your righteousness.

Psalm 145:4–7 NLT

I want to be part of sharing Your goodness with every generation, Lord. Help me boldly tell others about how awesome You are!

ANSWERS TO PRAYER

PRAYER REQUESTS

PRAISES

Friday, November 19

Each of you should use whatever gift you have received to serve others, as faithful stewards of God's grace in its various forms. If anyone speaks, they should do so as one who speaks the very words of God. If anyone serves, they should do so with the strength God provides, so that in all things God may be praised through Jesus Christ.

1 PETER 4:10–11 NIV

Father God, You are the giver of every ability, talent, and blessing I have. Help me to steward those gifts faithfully to bring glory and honor to You!

PRAYER REQUESTS

ANSWERS TO PRAYER

PRAISES

Saturday, November 20

"Everyone then who hears these words of mine and does them will be like a wise man who built his house on the rock. And the rain fell, and the floods came, and the winds blew and beat on that house, but it did not fall, because it had been founded on the rock."
MATTHEW 7:24–25 ESV

A solid and strong foundation—that's what I get when I live in Your wisdom and self-control. Thank You, Lord. I want to keep building well through Your Word.

ANSWERS TO PRAYER

PRAYER REQUESTS

PRAISES

Sunday, November 21

You, O Lord, are a God of compassion and mercy, slow to get angry and filled with unfailing love and faithfulness.
Psalm 86:15 NLT

Dear Lord, I admit I am quick to get angry sometimes. I'm not proud of that. Please forgive me and help me change. I'm so glad that You are slow to anger, and You offer unfailing love and faithfulness. I want to be more like You!

PRAYER REQUESTS

ANSWERS TO PRAYER

PRAISES

Monday, November 22

You have turned my mourning into joyful dancing. You have taken away my clothes of mourning and clothed me with joy, that I might sing praises to you and not be silent. O LORD my God, I will give you thanks forever!

PSALM 30:11–12 NLT

Only You, Lord! Only You could possibly turn mourning into joyful dancing. You give me purpose and peace, hope and life even during sorrow, struggle, and pain. I will never stop thanking and praising You!

ANSWERS TO PRAYER

PRAYER REQUESTS

PRAISES

Tuesday, November 23

The L*ORD's justice will dwell in the desert, his righteousness live in the fertile field. The fruit of that righteousness will be peace; its effect will be quietness and confidence forever. My people will live in peaceful dwelling places, in secure homes, in undisturbed places of rest.*

ISAIAH 32:16–18 NIV

Lord, I trust that heaven will be a forever paradise of peace. Until that day, fill me with Your peace during the challenges of life here on earth.

PRAYER REQUESTS

ANSWERS TO PRAYER

PRAISES

Wednesday, November 24

What good is it, dear brothers and sisters, if you say you have faith but don't show it by your actions? Can that kind of faith save anyone? Suppose you see a brother or sister who has no food or clothing, and you say, "Good-bye and have a good day; stay warm and eat well"—but then you don't give that person any food or clothing. What good does that do?

JAMES 2:14–16 NLT

Dear God, I want to prove my faith in You with my good and kind actions. Show me ways to help others and share Your truth.

ANSWERS TO PRAYER

PRAYER REQUESTS

PRAISES

Thursday, November 25

THANKSGIVING

Let them thank the LORD for his steadfast love, for his wondrous works to the children of man! For he satisfies the longing soul, and the hungry soul he fills with good things.

PSALM 107:8–9 ESV

Every day, but especially today, let us thank You, Lord. Your steadfast love truly satisfies. Every good thing we have ultimately comes from You. I am so very grateful!

PRAYER REQUESTS

ANSWERS TO PRAYER

PRAISES

Friday, November 26

I have not kept the good news of your justice hidden in my heart; I have talked about your faithfulness and saving power. I have told everyone in the great assembly of your unfailing love and faithfulness. Lord, don't hold back your tender mercies from me. Let your unfailing love and faithfulness always protect me.

Psalm 40:10–11 NLT

Lord, teach me to be bold in sharing about You and Your amazing love and faithfulness! Every person on the planet needs to hear about Your saving power. Use me to help make sure that happens.

PRAYER REQUESTS

ANSWERS TO PRAYER

PRAISES

Saturday, November 27

If any of you lacks wisdom, let him ask God, who gives generously to all without reproach, and it will be given him. But let him ask in faith, with no doubting, for the one who doubts is like a wave of the sea that is driven and tossed by the wind. For that person must not suppose that he will receive anything from the Lord; he is a double-minded man, unstable in all his ways.

James 1:5–8 ESV

Lord, please help me be self-controlled and stable through Your wisdom working in my life.

PRAYER REQUESTS

ANSWERS TO PRAYER

PRAISES

Sunday, November 28

If I had the gift of prophecy, and if I understood all of God's secret plans and possessed all knowledge, and if I had such faith that I could move mountains, but didn't love others, I would be nothing. . . . Three things will last forever—faith, hope, and love—and the greatest of these is love.

1 Corinthians 13:2, 13 NLT

Lord, remind me daily that all I do means nothing if I don't love others with Your great love as my source.

ANSWERS TO PRAYER

PRAYER REQUESTS

PRAISES

Monday, November 29

But don't just listen to God's word. You must do what it says. Otherwise, you are only fooling yourselves. . . . But if you look carefully into the perfect law that sets you free, and if you do what it says and don't forget what you heard, then God will bless you for doing it.

James 1:22–25 NLT

Lord, I want to remember every day that the highest joy isn't found in just sitting around and studying. It's in action, as I live out Your Word.

PRAYER REQUESTS

ANSWERS TO PRAYER

PRAISES

Tuesday, November 30

I remember your wonderful deeds of long ago. They are constantly in my thoughts. I cannot stop thinking about your mighty works. . . . You are the God of great wonders! You demonstrate your awesome power among the nations.

Psalm 77:11–14 NLT

Almighty God, when I focus on the wonderful deeds described in Your Word, plus the ways I see You working in the world today, plus the ways I've personally witnessed Your work—I can't help but be filled with peace. You've got this! Keep me constantly focused on all Your wonderful acts to fill me with peace.

ANSWERS TO PRAYER

PRAYER REQUESTS

PRAISES

DECEMBER 2027

O come, let us worship and bow down;
let us kneel before the Lord *our Maker.*
Psalm 95:6 skjv

SUNDAY	MONDAY	TUESDAY	WEDNESDAY	THURSDAY	FRIDAY	SATURDAY
			1	2	3	4
5	6	7	8	9	10	11
12	13	14	15	16	17	18
19	20	21 First Day of Winter	22	23	24 Christmas Eve / Hanukkah Begins at Sundown	25 Christmas Day
26	27	28	29	30	31 New Year's Eve	

As your December calendar fills with festivities of the season, take time at the beginning of the month to pause and set your heart on the coming Messiah. The Son of God who stepped down from heaven to live with us on earth is coming again to take us home to be with the Father!

Wednesday, December 1

Pure and genuine religion in the sight of God the Father means caring for orphans and widows in their distress and refusing to let the world corrupt you.

James 1:27 NLT

The love You pour out on my life is pure and perfect and whole, Father. Let it overflow into the lives of others. Make my love authentic and caring—always looking for ways to help those who are alone or isolated. And when those people benefit, I will give You the glory!

ANSWERS TO PRAYER

PRAYER REQUESTS

PRAISES

Thursday, December 2

"Why do you ask me about what is good?" Jesus replied. "There is only One who is good. If you want to enter life, keep the commandments."
MATTHEW 19:17 NIV

When I'm faced with a difficult choice, Father, I will look to You for direction. Your way is *always* good—always the best choice for me. Even if Your way seems difficult, give me the courage to take the first step, knowing You are there to help and sustain me along the way.

PRAYER REQUESTS

ANSWERS TO PRAYER

PRAISES

Friday, December 3

I want you to know that the Eternal your God is the only true God. He's the faithful God who keeps His covenants and shows loyal love for a thousand generations to those who in return love Him and keep His commands.

Deuteronomy 7:9 voice

Father, thank You for the faith of the people who came before me, who taught me about You. You have been faithful to Your family for generation after generation, and You won't stop!

ANSWERS TO PRAYER

PRAYER REQUESTS

PRAISES

Saturday, December 4

Put My yoke upon your shoulders—it might appear heavy at first, but it is perfectly fitted to your curves. Learn from Me, for I am gentle and humble of heart. When you are yoked to Me, your weary souls will find rest.

Matthew 11:29 voice

Jesus, You are always there for me, but You won't force Your will into my life. Keep reminding me that Your way, Your plan for me is perfect. Here, hand in hand with You, is where I find true rest and purpose.

PRAYER REQUESTS

ANSWERS TO PRAYER

PRAISES

Sunday, December 5

My little children, don't just talk about love as an idea or a theory. Make it your true way of life, and live in the pattern of gracious love.
1 John 3:18 voice

Most everyone—believers and nonbelievers alike—can agree that the world needs more love, Lord. But Your love is the only kind that brings true healing and lasting hope. Show me small steps to make Your love my way of life—every day in every way.

ANSWERS TO PRAYER

PRAYER REQUESTS

PRAISES

Monday, December 6

Make a joyful noise to the Lord, *all the earth! Serve the* Lord *with gladness! Come into his presence with singing!*

Psalm 100:1–2 esv

Lord, I will start today singing Your praises because I know the world wants to muffle my melody of worship. But I won't let it. . . I will find ways to praise no matter what! I choose gladness today because You love me, and I know You always will.

PRAYER REQUESTS

ANSWERS TO PRAYER

PRAISES

Tuesday, December 7

The work of being right and good will give peace.
From the right and good work will come quiet trust forever.
Isaiah 32:17 NLV

Lord, I constantly fight the temptation of sin—to make myself look better than I am, to tell a "harmless" lie to get ahead, to want more! But these choices leave me discontented and disappointed. I know that right living and following Your plan will lead to peace, both for me and the people around me. Help me live this way, Father!

ANSWERS TO PRAYER

PRAYER REQUESTS

PRAISES

Wednesday, December 8

Do not let kindness and truth leave you. Tie them around your neck. Write them upon your heart.

PROVERBS 3:3 NLV

The difficulties I endure have a way of distracting me from the good things You want for me, Lord. But I will not give up on being kind. I will not let go of Your truth and give in to the lies of the world. Holy Spirit, protect me from becoming jaded and cynical about my beliefs, and lead me in an abundant life of faith.

PRAYER REQUESTS

ANSWERS TO PRAYER

PRAISES

Thursday, December 9

We are allowed to do anything, but not everything is good for us to do. We are allowed to do anything, but not all things help us grow strong as Christians.

1 CORINTHIANS 10:23 NLV

I am thankful that many of the impossible-to-keep Old Testament laws are no longer part of my salvation story, Lord. I have so much freedom in You, but I need Your wisdom to know what I *should* do—what is most helpful and beneficial for my relationship with You!

ANSWERS TO PRAYER

PRAYER REQUESTS

PRAISES

Friday, December 10

"Do not be afraid of what you are about to suffer. I tell you, the devil will put some of you in prison to test you, and you will suffer persecution for ten days. Be faithful, even to the point of death, and I will give you life as your victor's crown."

REVELATION 2:10 NIV

The persecution the early Christians endured is scary to consider, Lord. As the world becomes less tolerant of You, please be near Your church and help us faithfully endure difficulties, standing for You.

PRAYER REQUESTS

ANSWERS TO PRAYER

PRAISES

Saturday, December 11

Always be humble and gentle. Be patient with each other, making allowance for each other's faults because of your love.
Ephesians 4:2 NLT

Humility, gentleness, and patience—these are three things I need more of, God! When I feel triggered by circumstances and people, remind me that it's because of Your loving-kindness toward me (especially when I don't deserve it) that I have learned to trust You. I'll do the same for others today.

ANSWERS TO PRAYER

PRAYER REQUESTS

PRAISES

Sunday, December 12

"This is My commandment, that you love one another as I have loved you."
John 15:12 SKJV

Thank You for loving me perfectly, powerfully, and unconditionally, Lord. To love others in that same way feels impossible! You don't expect perfection from me, Father, but rather, obedience. So today, help me to take small steps in loving others as You love me. Open my eyes to needs that I can meet in Your name.

PRAYER REQUESTS

ANSWERS TO PRAYER

PRAISES

Monday, December 13

But may all who search for you be filled with joy and gladness in you.
May those who love your salvation repeatedly shout, "God is great!"
PSALM 70:4 NLT

God, You *are* great! You are more to me than I can put into words. In You I find my hope and purpose and joy. I praise You for Your goodness, for Your majesty, for Your strength, Your power, and Your *greatness*!

ANSWERS TO PRAYER

PRAYER REQUESTS

PRAISES

Tuesday, December 14

To the highest heights of the universe, glory to God! And on earth, peace among all people who bring pleasure to God!
Luke 2:14 voice

Jesus, I long for Your peace—especially during this time of year. But the calendar is filled with events and obligations, and the busyness of the season sometimes robs me of that peace. This year, help me pause and reflect on the miracle of Your life on earth as Emmanuel—God with us!

PRAYER REQUESTS

ANSWERS TO PRAYER

PRAISES

Wednesday, December 15

Think of the kindness you wish others would show you; do the same for them.
Luke 6:31 voice

Some days I'm completely blind to everything but my own frustrations, Lord. That's when I tend to feel isolated and without hope. Give me Your eyes, Father. Help me look outward and find someone else to show Your kindness to. When I elevate others, You elevate me!

ANSWERS TO PRAYER

PRAYER REQUESTS

PRAISES

Thursday, December 16

Who is wise and understanding among you? Let them show it by their good life, by deeds done in the humility that comes from wisdom.
James 3:13 NIV

If there's one thing I want more of, God, it's Your wisdom. Help me discern what You want as I study Your Word and learn more about Your will and ways. Give me discernment to see people and circumstances through Your eyes, and show me the wisdom that comes with humble, modest living.

PRAYER REQUESTS

ANSWERS TO PRAYER

PRAISES

Friday, December 17

If we confess our sins, he is faithful and just to forgive us our sins and to cleanse us from all unrighteousness.

1 John 1:9 ESV

I'm here. . .*again*. . .asking for Your forgiveness, Father. I get so frustrated with myself for returning to sin, to wrong choices, to the pitfalls I desperately want to avoid. Yet Your Word says You will faithfully forgive me and make me right with You. Thank You for not giving up on me.

ANSWERS TO PRAYER

PRAYER REQUESTS

PRAISES

Saturday, December 18

Keep your gentle nature so that all people will know what it looks like to walk in His footsteps. The Lord is ever present with us.
Philippians 4:5 voice

Father, forgive me for buying into the world's lie that strength and gentleness can't exist in the same person. *You*, Lord, are both! Show me, more and more each day, how to live this out as Jesus did on earth.

PRAYER REQUESTS

ANSWERS TO PRAYER

PRAISES

Sunday, December 19

"God expressed His love for the world in this way:
He gave His only Son so that whoever believes in Him will not
face everlasting destruction, but will have everlasting life."
John 3:16 voice

Father God, the swaddled newborn in the nativity reminds me that You sent Your Son—from the safety of Your side in heaven—to the fallen, sinful earth. You watched as Jesus faced wrongful accusations and murder. Then You raised Him to life—all for Your glory and my eternity. That is love!

ANSWERS TO PRAYER

PRAYER REQUESTS

PRAISES

Monday, December 20

The angel said to them, "Do not be afraid. I bring you good news that will cause great joy for all the people."
LUKE 2:10 NIV

Jesus, Your good news of great joy is for everyone—not just people who look like me, think like me, and act like me. The world notices Your bright light more this time of year. I will use Christmastime as an opportunity to share Your love and the gift of Your grace with others.

PRAYER REQUESTS

ANSWERS TO PRAYER

PRAISES

Tuesday, December 21

FIRST DAY OF WINTER

For to us a Child will be born. To us a Son will be given. And the rule of the nations will be on His shoulders. His name will be called Wonderful, Teacher, Powerful God, Father Who Lives Forever, Prince of Peace.

Isaiah 9:6 NLV

You are the King of my heart, Jesus, and my Prince of Peace. Cover me with Your grace today so I can experience Your power, Your might, and Your forgiveness that saves me and promises me eternity with You!

ANSWERS TO PRAYER

PRAYER REQUESTS

PRAISES

Wednesday, December 22

Let us not become weary in doing good, for at the proper time we will reap a harvest if we do not give up.
GALATIANS 6:9 NIV

Choosing to do good isn't always the easiest option, Lord. Yet I know that choosing to love, to encourage, to lighten a load, to show others Your grace—these are things You honor and bless. When doing good seems too hard, remind me that You are present in those good things, and with You is where I want to be!

PRAYER REQUESTS

ANSWERS TO PRAYER

PRAISES

Thursday, December 23

"If you sinful people know how to give good gifts to your children, how much more will your heavenly Father give good gifts to those who ask him."
MATTHEW 7:11 NLT

I find so much joy in giving gifts at Christmas, Lord—*especially* giving gifts to the children in my life. It's encouraging to know that You love giving me good gifts even more! Thank You for the unending blessings I see in my past and present, and for Your goodness I know will continue in the future.

ANSWERS TO PRAYER

PRAYER REQUESTS

PRAISES

Friday, December 24

CHRISTMAS EVE / HANUKKAH BEGINS AT SUNDOWN

The Word (Christ) was in the beginning. The Word was with God. The Word was God. He was with God in the beginning.

JOHN 1:1–2 NLV

I worship You, my Savior and God, because You have been the beloved Son since before the dawn of time. You have always been, You are, and You always will be. When I have moments of doubt and worry, Lord, remind me of Your unending, rock-solid presence, protection, and love.

PRAYER REQUESTS

PRAISES

ANSWERS TO PRAYER

Saturday, December 25

CHRISTMAS DAY

Avoiding a fight is a mark of honor; only fools insist on quarreling.
PROVERBS 20:3 NLT

Father, I love my family so much, but sometimes big holidays feel like a keg of TNT just waiting for a lit fuse. When tensions and expectations run high, I want to be a peacemaker among the people I love. Help me hold my tongue and work at avoiding fights. I want Your love to define our celebrations.

ANSWERS TO PRAYER

PRAYER REQUESTS

PRAISES

Sunday, December 26

Let love prevail in your life, words, and actions.
1 Corinthians 16:14 voice

Show me, Lord, how to cover every part of my life in Your love. I want to inhale Your goodness and exhale care and concern around me. Help me understand Your heart as I read Your Word, so I can speak love every time I open my mouth. Show me Your work in my life so I can emulate that in how I treat others.

PRAYER REQUESTS

ANSWERS TO PRAYER

PRAISES

Monday, December 27

"You will not leave my soul among the dead or allow your Holy One to rot in the grave. You have shown me the way of life, and you will fill me with the joy of your presence."
Acts 2:27–28 NLT

Before I knew You, Lord, I couldn't have imagined the joy You would bring into my life. The world desperately needs this infusion of true hope and joy. Use me to show others the way to You so they can find it!

ANSWERS TO PRAYER

PRAYER REQUESTS

PRAISES

Tuesday, December 28

The kingdom of God is not a matter of eating and drinking but of righteousness and peace and joy in the Holy Spirit.
ROMANS 14:17 ESV

When the temporary things of this world distract me from You, God, may Your Spirit guide me back to truth. . .to the things that matter. I want to live an upright life that spreads Your peace and joy in every conversation and relationship.

PRAYER REQUESTS

ANSWERS TO PRAYER

PRAISES

Wednesday, December 29

If we look forward to something we don't yet have,
we must wait patiently and confidently.
ROMANS 8:25 NLT

Father, I come to you every day with requests. I've been asking for certain things for a long time, but I refuse to get discouraged because I haven't received them yet. I am confident that You hear my prayers, Lord, and that in Your time You will answer according to Your will. Please give me patience and hope as I wait.

ANSWERS TO PRAYER

PRAYER REQUESTS

PRAISES

Thursday, December 30

Make every effort to add to your faith goodness; and to goodness, knowledge.
2 Peter 1:5 NIV

When I'm tempted to think I have all the faith I need, Lord, remind me that You will continue to work on me until I join You in heaven. While there is still breath in my lungs, I have more to learn about You. Teach me Your goodness and wisdom. Make me righteous. Show me how to truly love others as You love me.

PRAYER REQUESTS

PRAISES

ANSWERS TO PRAYER

Friday, December 31

NEW YEAR'S EVE

If we have no faith, He will still be faithful for He cannot go against what He is.
2 TIMOTHY 2:13 NLV

Your commitment to me is not dependent on my faithfulness, Lord. This is a comforting yet humbling truth. I *want* to be faithfully committed to You, Father, yet I still make bad choices and sin, breaking that right standing with You. Thank You for being the rock that doesn't move in my life. I will cling to Your promise to always love me!

ANSWERS TO PRAYER

PRAYER REQUESTS

PRAISES

Notes

Contributors

Annie Barkley made up her first story at the ripe old age of two when she asked her mom to write it down for her. Since then she has read and written many words as a student, newspaper reporter, author, and editor. She has a passion for making God's Word come to life for readers through devotions and Bible study. Annie loves snow (which is a good thing because she lives in Ohio), wearing scarves, eating sushi, playing Scrabble, and spending time with friends and family. Annie wrote entries for February, April, June, August, October, and December.

JoAnne Simmons is a writer and editor who's in awe of God's love and the ways He guides and provides. Her favorite things include coffee shops, libraries, the Bible, good grammar, being a wife and mom, dogs, music, Disney World, punctuation, church, the beach, and many dear family and friends—but not in that order. If her family weren't so loving and flexible, she'd be in big trouble; and if God's mercies weren't new every morning, she'd never get out of bed. JoAnne wrote entries for January, March, May, July, September, and November.